"Effectively partnering with subject matter experts in instructional design projects is one of the critical skills a designer must develop. Yet most instructional design training programs place far less emphasis on this competency than they do on issues like objective writing, the ADDIE model, adult learning, and other ISD concepts. Dr. Hodell takes a methodical approach in defining and developing the various SME relationships and successfully incorporating them into the ISD process. As with all of Dr. Hodell's books, this provides tools and specific processes that are immediately useful. The discussion question/case study construct at the end of each chapter is something we will use for our ongoing training of staff development."

Todd Brace
Director of Corporate Learning
Medifast

"Dr. Chuck Hodell strikes gold again! Recognizing the critically important role of subject matter experts (SMEs) in today's increasingly complex training and instructional design field, Dr. Hodell provides a highly practical resource. A veritable buffet of goodies, this text begins with an introductory chapter on the types and roles of SMEs. Subsequent chapters tackle important topics such as managing SMEs, introducing SMEs to instructional design, and more advanced topics such as evaluating the performance of an SME and solving common problems that may arise. The last chapter is a gem all by itself—a robust discussion of what to do, and not to do when working with SMEs. As promised by the title, this text provides a "no-nonsense approach" to partnering with SMEs. A must for the bookshelf of every instructional designer!"

Dr. Mary Lynn McPherson
Professor and Vice Chair for Education
University of Maryland School of Pharmacy

"In today's fast-paced, digital age society where face-to-face and online collaborations grow increasingly challenging and diverse, Hodell once again presents a practical and much needed guide for instructional designers. Trainers, designers, and subject matter experts will all benefit from Hodell's expert advice and proven strategies that lead to efficient and successful partnerships between professionals."

Erica C. Boling, PhD
Associate Professor
Rutgers, The State University of New Jersey

SMEs
From the Ground Up

A No-Nonsense Approach to
Trainer-Expert Collaboration

Chuck Hodell

ASTD PRESS

ASTD Press is an internationally renowned source of insightful and practical information on workplace learning, performance, and professional development.

ASTD Press
1640 King Street Box 1443
Alexandria, VA 22313-1443 USA

Ordering information: Books published by ASTD Press can be purchased by visiting ASTD's website at store.astd.org or by calling 800.628.2783 or 703.683.8100.

Library of Congress Control Number: 2013931621
ISBN-10: 1-56286-855-1
ISBN-13: 978-1-56286-855-0
e-ISBN: 978-1-60728-667-7

ASTD Press Editorial Staff:
Director: Glenn Saltzman
Manager, ASTD Press: Ashley McDonald
Community of Practice Manager, Learning and Development: Juana Llorens
Associate Editor: Heidi Smith
Editorial Assistant: Sarah Cough
Text and Cover Design: Marisa Kelly
Printed by: Victor Graphics, Inc., Baltimore, MD, www.victorgraphics.com

Table of Contents

Introduction vii

Chapter 1 The Subject Matter Expert's Role in Training and ISD 1

Chapter 2 Selecting Technical SMEs 15

Chapter 3 TSME Committee Structure 31

Chapter 4 Welcoming SMEs to the Process 45

Chapter 5 Defining Roles and Responsibilities 57

Chapter 6 Versions, Deliverables, and Deadlines 69

Chapter 7 Evaluating SME Performance 77

Chapter 8 Problem Solving in SME Committees 95

Chapter 9 ISD Boot Camp for SMEs 105

Chapter 10 Migrating SMEs Into Mainstream Training and ISD Roles 117

Chapter 11 SME Dos and Don'ts 123

Acknowledgments 137

About the Author 139

Index 141

Introduction

The roles of trainer and instructional designer have never been more diverse and challenging than today. The demands placed on ISD professionals mirror the changes taking place across every inch of the learning landscape, from social media and new technologies, to more efficient work practices and procedures.

From nonprofits to multinationals, the emphasis on training has grown exponentially as organizations realize that investments in the training function represent the most efficient and cost-effective avenue for maintaining and expanding skills, updating and supporting new products and services, and providing the mandated training required in today's regulatory environment. Instructional design is suddenly "new" again, and with it comes the attention to best practice and efficiency that only a systems approach to training can provide.

As the need for training has grown, so has the need for an expanded family of professionals required to design and implement training. At no time in the past has the role of subject matter experts (SMEs) been more important, or grown so rapidly. SMEs are the heart of many instructional design projects, and trainers have struggled for years to find the best way to incorporate this highly talented group of professionals into the design family.

As a college professor, students are as likely to ask me about how to work with SMEs as they are to ask about how to write great objectives or design online learning. There seems to be a real vacuum of best practices and approaches to working with SMEs. Since instructional design and training now thrive on getting content correct, there is no realistic way to do this efficiently and productively without finding the best way to work with SMEs.

I started in training as a subject matter expert, and outside of my roles in training and instructional design, I still serve as an SME in some content areas. I am guessing the same is true for most of you. The world of traditional training responsibilities and the important role that SMEs hold are not mutually exclusive. They in fact thrive when working together.

My early experiences with SMEs as an instructional designer and project manager were both challenging and rewarding. I remember the first time I hired one of my former college professors as a content expert, and had to manage that relationship with all its inherent awkwardness. There was also the time I was given a month's notice that I was going to manage a massive skilled-trades design project that was to start with five committees of SMEs, all arriving on the same day to work on five different content areas. We started that project with 30 SMEs, five instructional designers, and a flipchart. Several years later, the group of training modules was well beyond 250 designed and implemented internationally.

I survived these and hundreds of other similar challenges because I quickly learned that a talented content expert could be just as rich an asset as the best instructional designer or facilitator. Every aspect of your relationship with SMEs is just as important as every other project-related relationship you have, and there shouldn't be any value system that suggests any of these elements is more important than another. And, that's the point. The magic in working with SMEs is as much common sense and relationship-building as it is any other skills. I have never felt more challenged or worked harder than the times I was bringing a design project to fruition shoulder to shoulder with the best and brightest in a given content area and a team of first-class trainers and designers.

As a result of those years of experience and the assistance and guidance of thousands of SMEs and talented instructional designers, I offer you some insights into what I have learned the hard way. I have also asked a select group of SMEs and designers their thoughts on this relationship, and their ideas appear in every chapter of this volume.

Hopefully with this book you will learn how to work most efficiently with SMEs and how to nurture training and design skills within SMEs to the mutual benefit of both groups. Many trainers were first SMEs, and it isn't much of a leap for motivated, smart SMEs to become key players in the design and implementation of courses.

No matter your level of experience in training at this point, this book will provide the basics of building a productive working relationship with SMEs, and it will also offer hundreds of tips on building great courses by incorporating the talents of SMEs in the course design process itself. Not only can you benefit from the subject matter knowledge they bring to the process, you can also move SMEs toward the training and instructional design side of the equation in ways that benefit all aspects of the process.

My suggestions for ways to use this book are based on my belief that each of you is in a different place in your career and the context of your work may or may not be similar to anyone else. For those just starting in training and design, you may gain the greatest value with a complete read of this book to get a general feel for the relationship between SMEs and trainers. It will serve as a starting point for your more specific needs and interests. If you are an experienced professional, you may find that specific chapters—as outlined below—offer a new insight or approach to an existing challenge. You may find new job responsibilities that you hadn't considered before.

Everyone should read **chapter 1**. In this chapter, you will find important foundational information about SMEs and their roles in training. You will find out about the earliest SMEs and how they evolved to their important roles in today's training environment. There are five different types of SMEs in training, and you'll see why it is important to recognize these different roles when working with SMEs.

If you are responsible for selecting and managing SMEs, the information in **chapter 2** will be key to making great SME selections and managing this vital resource. You will review the elements to look for in SMEs, and you can see how to rate the skills of individual SMEs with very objective data points, ranging from skill-specific elements to more general "ability to work in a team environment" elements. Don't miss this chapter if you want to find out what separates the average from the excellent in SMEs.

One of the most difficult assignments any trainer can face is the prospect of forming and managing a group of SMEs. **Chapter 3** walks you through the three types of structures these SME committees generally take, and how to select leaders among your SMEs. Learn how to build a supporting environment for your SMEs that allows them to thrive while working with you.

One valuable element of working with SMEs that most novices miss is the importance of welcoming SMEs to a project and the world of training and design. **Chapter 4** provides an overview of different elements in the process to consider, and offers examples of ways to do this effectively.

As your work with SMEs becomes more detailed, you will find value in acting on the need for role development within your SME groups. In **chapter 5**, you'll be able to make sure that each SME knows the role she plays in the process, and how to ensure that your SMEs work well together in support of your project.

If you have ever worked on a training project where versioning, deliverables, and deadlines became a problem, you will find comfort in **chapter 6**, since working with SMEs and not having a plan for these issues only makes the problems exponentially worse. It is bad enough to have the wrong version of a deliverable if only one or two trainers are working with it. Imagine (or revisit) the problems associated with many SMEs all working on different versions of a deliverable. You will find useful ideas here for this universally challenging situation.

Most of us dread the idea that we have to evaluate someone's performance and take action or make recommendations based on what we find. This often leads to a complete denial of this process and later negative consequences. In **chapter 7**, you will find a complete rubric of elements to consider when evaluating SME performance, including an objective-based rating scale. Some of you will find this interesting but not actionable in your situation, but knowing what to look for is useful, regardless of any eventual action on your part.

The more experienced reader will find the problem-solving elements in **chapter 8** useful when you have SME issues that need to be addressed. These can be generated from some sort of evaluation process (either similar to the model in chapter 7 or one of your own design), or from complaints of other SMEs or training staff. This chapter helps identify some common problems you may experience, and offers suggestions for addressing them.

If you have ever felt the need to provide instructional systems development (ISD) training to your SMEs, **chapter 9** is the place to start. Here you will find an outline for a boot camp-type training and also common questions and answers that many SMEs ask about the process of designing training. There is also a short glossary of training and ISD terms to share with SMEs.

Once you have given your SMEs a background on ISD and training, you may find some of these experts are interested in becoming more permanently engaged in the training process. **Chapter 10** offers some ideas for supporting and nurturing SMEs who want to move to the world of training and design.

The final chapter in this book is a resource for all trainers and designers who work with SMEs. **Chapter 11** is a series of "Dos and Don'ts" gathered from conversations with experienced trainers and instructional designers with more than two hundred years of experience working with SMEs. The voices of SMEs who have offered their insight into being on the SME side are also reflected here.

When you are finished reading, I hope that you use this book as a desk reference for ideas and approaches as you work through your specific roles. One size does not fit all, and at no point would I ever recommend you simply accept my ideas without modifying them to fit the reality of your situation. Start here and take ownership of these ideas in your own unique way.

Chapter 1

The Subject Matter Expert's Role in Training and ISD

Chapter Objectives

At the end of chapter 1, you will be able to:

- Define an SME in the context of the training environment.
- Describe at least three different roles SMEs play in training.
- List and describe the characteristics of five different types of SMEs utilized in training.

Chapter Overview

Defining what an SME is in the modern era of instructional design requires moving past the traditional ideas about SMEs. We can promote real progress by engaging and incorporating this important asset into our training family. Recognizing that SMEs exist in all disciplines—and that a content expert is the same as a graphic artist or programmer working on a project—opens unlimited avenues of cooperation and communication. The training professional who embraces this emerging concept reflects the new generation of practice that lifts instructional design to a new level of efficiency and standards.

SMEs

The single most misunderstood and mismanaged asset in training and curriculum development is the SME. From time immemorial they have proved an enigma to generations of training professionals. Like Professor Moriarty was to Sherlock Holmes, they may prove to be a constant riddle to our best instincts, yet they are irreplaceable in our work. They make us better trainers and designers in areas no other resource can even remotely hope to influence, while still nudging us toward a higher level of achievement in our broad role.

Some of my most satisfying work in training has been the countless hours spent in the company of really bright and energetic content professionals working on a project. Their energy and enthusiasm has buoyed me in times of doubt and supported me in times of less than brilliant decisions. They have also proved to be my biggest challenge, as their level of achievement and knowledge demand my best, and anything less is obvious to all involved. Through it all, you quickly learn that SMEs are no different from you. As a professional, you have certain expectations and admire certain qualities in others you work with. So it is with content experts, and so it has been for generations of trainers.

> **They have also proved to be my biggest challenge, as their level of achievement and knowledge demand my best, and anything less is obvious to all involved.**

SMEs are certainly not a new phenomenon—far from it. For countless centuries, experts in every aspect of life and work have shared their knowledge with others in an effort to enlighten the less informed on every imaginable topic. From the earliest voices forging oral histories and telling stories, to the digital storytelling resident in social media, the passing of knowledge has been an admired and cherished endeavor from the beginning of recorded history.

Beginning roughly 32,000 years ago, the first recorded training consisted of cave drawings that depicted which animals were safe to eat. In this way, tribe members could consult the walls of the caves to learn from those who came before how to safely feed themselves. This passing of knowledge from an SME to a learner has changed little in the intervening tens of thousands of years.

When you think about it, it would be difficult to learn anything at all without someone sharing what they have learned with you and others. To paraphrase Isaac Newton, we all stand on the shoulders of giants when we gain new knowledge. All of this knowledge is passed to us by someone who has learned and shared that information to those who followed. It wasn't until recently that we had a name for this knowledge sharer in the training world: SMEs.

Defining SMEs

As we begin our discussion of SMEs, we need to agree on how to define an SME and the roles they play in our training work. As you will soon see, there is no one single definition or type of SME. While most in our work of designing training are content-related SMEs, others are process-related SMEs, like writers and programmers.

SME is the universal designation for any individual who is considered to be an expert in one or more areas of endeavor. This expertise can be in content areas such as math or science, or a professional field such as law or accounting—or as we will see shortly, an SME can also be a key noncontent member of a training or instructional design team.

When we describe a content SME, or a technical subject matter expert (TSME), the term can accurately apply to a building trades crafts-worker with 40 years of experience hanging iron atop the world's highest buildings, or a village elder with no formal education sharing centuries-old herbal treatments for common ailments. The 14-year-old next door is an SME in the latest musical genre, and a 92-year-old World War II veteran will serve as an expert on the Battle of Stalingrad, which happened in 1942. In all cases, the SME provides specific, detailed information that is not considered to be common knowledge among a general population. No two SMEs look the same or sound alike, and there may be no other defining element besides their related subject matter knowledge.

SMEs earn this standing in countless ways depending on the circumstances surrounding their knowledge. Some have years of experience in a field and have written articles or books, and may teach or offer seminars in a specific field. Others may be recognized by their peers as the "best of the best" and earn the SME title by virtue of their reputation. A minority of people are self-proclaimed SMEs and offer little in the way of credentialing to substantiate their expertise. It is also sometimes a subjective art to label someone (or yourself) as an SME. There is no group called the International Order of Subject Matter Experts that crowns the worthy few with this credential.

For our purposes in training, a TSME has generally passed the associated litmus tests within their field. This is often based on academic achievement, licensure and certification, publishing in the field, or some other formal credentialing process. There should always be an experience component to ensure that even the best educational credentialing is supported by years of actual practice in a field. In some professions, the yearly in-service training required to continue licensure or credentialing supports SME status.

The title of SME should not be given without credentials that match the practice among professionals in a specific area. Many times these are also the generally accepted entry points for professional practice. In academic circles, this is generally a terminal degree like a PhD or EdD. In law, it is a license to practice law and perhaps a JD degree. In medicine, it is a terminal degree like an MD or DO and board certification. In the building trades, this can be journey-person status and having many years of experience as an apprenticeship instructor. The examples go on and really have no limit. It is important that there is some tangible, reliable, and documented evidence to support "expert" standing.

The Genius Factor

There are notable exceptions to these common standards and accepted guidelines. Without question, we occasionally encounter uniquely gifted individuals who represent the outliers in this labeling process. Musical prodigies like Mozart or Chopin join Enrico Fermi in physics, Bill Gates in software design, and Steve Jobs at Apple, all of whom unquestionably defied accepted definitions of "expert" at some point early in their careers. To apply a strict, credential-based standard to any of these geniuses would be laughable, and yet there are still some who argue the "line in the sand" standard must always be supported. Be open to some reasonable interpretation of this definition in your work.

The Irony

As trainers and instructional designers, the irony in all of this is that we are also SMEs. We are SMEs in our chosen profession in the same way that our colleagues in other fields are content experts in theirs. It is the context that changes when we work with other content experts.

Rather than look at SMEs utilized during the curriculum design process as outsiders, it is a much more productive and mutually beneficial standard of practice to think of everyone on a project as an expert SME. In this way, we all share the same professional space and remove any traces of boundaries or artificial barriers that affect our work and eventual success.

For this book, the terms SME and content expert are synonymous when referring to technical subject matter experts (TSMEs). However, not all SMEs are content experts, as you will soon discover. There are several other terms that cover the same semantic territory, and don't be surprised by some of the terms different groups use. They are all the same for our purposes, except in how we define the different subsets of SMEs, as you will see later.

Why SMEs Are Important to ISD

Often the term SME is tossed into a conversation as if it is just one single entity or function. As we have already discussed, it isn't, and the more you know about SMEs, the more important they become to your success. Best practice in ISD demands that SMEs take their rightful place as part of the design family with equal expectations and responsibilities as other people in the process.

The rapid maturation of instructional design over the last decade has curiously allowed a vacuum in the appreciation and integration of SMEs in the design team. This may be linked to a heightened focus on the key process elements of training and instructional design, whether represented by the ADDIE model elements of analysis, design, development, implementation, and evaluation—or other priorities, like online learning and social media.

This unenlightened view of SMEs is not intentional, but is nonetheless detrimental, since it minimizes the potential benefits of incorporating this asset where most useful. In a professional practice that strives on thoroughness and attention to detail, SMEs often languish as a disassociated element in the practice of ISD. In truth, they are often as essential to success as any other factor in our work.

SMEs in Training Occupations

It is difficult to find anyone associated with training and curriculum design who was not first involved in a non-training field, and by default, most likely an SME in something other than training and curriculum design. The same can be said for almost everyone holding the title of trainer, teacher, facilitator, professor, or various other coaching and mentoring roles. From the earliest oral traditions in education and training, skills and knowledge were passed from the most proficient to those following them.

Almost all academic programs teaching instructional design and learning and performance are offered to people who have experience in something other than training and education, and are now advancing their careers by learning more about the finer points of designing and implementing training. The ASTD Certified Professional in Learning and Performance (CPLP) certification is a perfect example of the transitional nature of skills in training from SMEs who work in a variety of professions to becoming a learning and performance SME. The University of Maryland Baltimore County Master's degree and graduate certificate programs in instructional systems development do not have any requirements for prior experience or a specific undergraduate degree.

It is this path from SME to training role that has the potential to create uncertainty, since there are assumptions that someone who is good in one area of endeavor is also good in another. This questionable nexus between an individual's content expertise and their more general training or instructional design knowledge invites conflicted role perceptions and opens the door to the possibility of dysfunctional committees, groups, and projects.

SMEs generally work and fit best in the role of an SME. To expect more of them is to invite a variety of potentially negative consequences. At the same time, when an SME attempts to expand their role into an area that interferes with established non-SME roles, it may create equally negative results. It is the balance of role and expectation that creates the best and most productive fit in this environment. So going beyond the simplistic one-size-fits-all definition for SMEs works to our advantage.

SMEs Are More Than Just Content Experts

The commonly accepted definition of the term SME is universally linked to an individual who has specific content knowledge in a defined field. We have SMEs in every imaginable content area, from alligators to zebras. This definition has served us well for thousands of years, but it is now time to move past this legacy view of SMEs in the field of training and instructional design.

As we have already learned, the term and classification of SME includes every professional partner in our training enterprise. Later in the chapter, we will see that SMEs are both content-related and process-related. The programmer, the writer, the teacher/trainer, and the manager are also SMEs in ways that matter in our work. Identifying and working with all of these specific types of SMEs provides endless possibilities for improved products and processes.

Imagine that you are designing a training program in one of the fields that a member of our training partnership represents. If you were designing a program for new writers, wouldn't you have an established writer as an SME? And a new course in working with learning management systems (LMS) would need an SME in LMS design. And on and on. Once you start to think about all established professionals as SMEs, your mindset changes and opportunities arise to create better working relationships with this other SME family.

Categorizing SMEs in Training

You now know that in training the term SME encompasses many different roles and responsibilities, and this amalgamation renders the term almost meaningless without further clarification. When trainers experience confusion and frustration in their relationships with SMEs, it may at least partially come from the fact that we haven't moved passed the stereotype to find the best fit for each different type of SME. Each project is different, as is each SME, but it is always worth the time to sort out what you have and figure out how to best utilize these talented professionals.

Given our need for clarity and avenues to efficiency and quality, it serves training best to define the primary categories of SMEs as technical, hybrid, instructional, functional, and sentinel. Each has a very distinct purpose and responsibility.

Figure 1-1: Types of SMEs

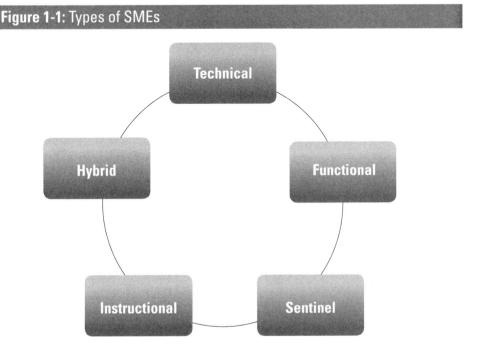

Technical SME

If you asked a hundred trainers to define a generic SME, what a majority would probably describe is a technical subject matter expert (TSME). As the name implies, a TSME provides the technical component in training. Many times this individual is the seasoned professional who shares his knowledge of a particular area of specialty, and that becomes the core content in a course.

These are master craftspeople, engineers, scientists, lawyers, physicians, biologists, electricians, human resource professionals, or anyone who has a demonstrated subject matter expertise to enhance curriculum development. You may find your TSMEs don't have a lot of experience with the training design process and are appointed to these positions with or without their knowledge or approval. It is often true that any assignments related to their role as a TSME are in addition to their regular job responsibilities, and this may become a point of contention. In other cases, TSMEs are consultants who work on many of these projects and are very familiar with their role and function.

The focus in this book is our work with TSMEs, but the same principles apply to all of our SME categories. We spend more time with this group than any other because this group is more common, and it is easy to apply all of our experience to each SME type.

Table 1-1: Technical SME

Technical SME
• content expert
• professional standing
• demonstrated expertise
• design support only

Hybrid SME

In some training and education settings, numerous factors may require professionals to consolidate duties and engage in more than one training role. This hybrid subject matter expert (HSME) both participates in the design of a course and also implements the course once designed. This unique set of skills has its own challenges that must be recognized and addressed.

In higher education, the HSME is the rule rather than the exception, and HSMEs are generally stronger in content knowledge and weaker in designing courses. This becomes especially noticeable when courses move online, either in a blended mix of online and classroom or in a full online course. It is a very difficult transition to move from designing courses based primarily on lecture and systematic evaluations to designing courses using ISD.

The HSME is also a very standard category when working with apprenticeship and other highly technical content areas. It is common for the best-skilled trade person to be brought in to teach others. This is how we gather most of our HSMEs for designing skills training.

Table 1-2: Hybrid SME

Hybrid SME
• content expert
• professional standing
• demonstrated expertise
• design and implementation

Instructional SME

The role of facilitator, mentor, coach, and teacher are all included in the instructional subject matter expert (ISME) category. While this group possesses vast subject matter expertise, their primary role is to enhance the instructional aspects of the training during implementation. It is not unusual for a technical course to be taught by an ISME that does not participate in the design, development, or management of the training. Still, their technical expertise is key to their ability to facilitate or enhance the learning experience.

Table 1-3: Instructional SME

Instructional SME
• trainer/teacher
• implements design products
• content knowledge supports implementation

Functional SME

In multiple training environments, there are many SMEs who have little to do with building the content in a course, but contribute in ways that enhance the final product. While seldom involved in forming the content itself, their skills are unique to training and should be recognized as such.

A functional subject matter expert (FSME) might be a graphic artist, programmer, web designer, technical writer, photographer, or any other associated professional. The recognition of an individual's expertise goes a long way in defining and building this role in the training function. We seldom think of these skills in the context of subject matter expertise, but they possess all of the qualities we seek in an SME, and to bring them into this discussion enhances our ability to build a winning training function.

Almost no one considers these professionals as SMEs in an instructional design context, and taking the time to consider the importance of the designation works to your favor. This group is proud of their work and they seldom get any recognition beyond the usual internal team appreciation. However, once you think of them as SMEs, you change the way you work with them in important ways.

As a group, they deserve the same respect and treatment as the content-related SMEs, and all of the ideas presented in this book apply equally to them in the context of their work and role in your project. Making them part of your team and not just an adjunct participating on the margins will bring tangible results over time. Don't ignore this group and don't take them for granted. They can negate any advantage you have gained with your other SME groups if they are left unappreciated and unrecognized as SMEs.

Table 1-4: Functional SME

Functional SME
• support professional function
• graphic artist, writer, and so on
• no content knowledge

Sentinel SME

In the world of training, the sentinel subject matter expert (SSME) is the individual who serves as the overseer or guardian of the content while designing and implementing courseware. This individual may possess limited and often dated technical expertise, but he serves in the managerial role of reviewing and approving content related to design and implementation of the final training product.

They are considered SMEs because they ensure that the content and product meet—and hopefully exceed—expected professional and organizational standards. And, while their content-specific knowledge might be limited, they still have the organizational responsibility to act as sentinel for both content and process. In training and instructional design, the SSME must be treated differently than any other participant in the process. Their knowledge of the content places them in a unique organizational situation: They may experience pressure from several directions when making important decisions, since those they report to might have priorities different from those related to training and to their role as an SME.

This group can be especially challenging, since their first priority is not necessarily the content. In most cases they are concerned with budget and deliverables rather than with specific content issues of the designed material. They will endlessly churn the most miniscule budget item, and they want answers when a deadline is missed. While genuinely concerned about the content, they have higher authorities to appease, and those authorities have limited knowledge of project and process details. When working with this group, make sure you have all of your facts in order and make sure you have answers for even the smallest details related to budget and deadlines.

SSMEs really appreciate and respond to having tangible items to review and share with those higher in the organizational food chain. As professionals, they have grown weary and suspicious of anything they can't see or hold in their hands. Trying to float something by this group is impossible. Have copies of every deliverable ready for them to review. Make sure they have timelines and budgets ad nauseam, and always appear to have much more information for them than they will ever have time to review.

Another helpful approach in working with this group is to have TSMEs talk about their work and share insights on how the project is going (assuming it is going well). SSMEs really pay attention when the SMEs that they have assigned to work on a project talk about their success. This allows the SSMEs to take away a feeling of accomplishment, and they can then float this success higher in the organization.

Of all of the SMEs you work with, this group above all others has to feel comfortable with your leadership and the investment they are making in a project. If they are happy, most other levels of the process will respond positively to your facilitation—if for no other reason than because they know the sentinels are satisfied with the way things are progressing.

Table 1-5: Sentinel SME

Sentinel SME
• oversees course design from a distance • limited or dated content knowledge • assures quality and related organizational concerns

Matching SME Types and Your Needs

Categorizing subject matter expertise provides several advantages in training, not the least of which is the ability to find the best and most efficient way to incorporate these valuable assets in each individual training environment. It's really a matter of respect and appreciation for the time and effort that these professionals invest in making our training successful.

In order to best utilize our valuable SMEs, we need to first identify what we need from them and when we need it. Using the ADDIE model of ISD (more in chapter 9) as our guide, there are certain elements of the process that best suit themselves to the different types of SMEs.

In table 1-6, we can see that each element of ADDIE has a specific need for SMEs. Each classification of SME will likely fit best within particular ADDIE elements. While each project is different, these are generally appropriate associations.

Table 1-6: SMEs and ISD Elements

	Analysis	Design	Development	Implementation	Evaluation
Technical	X	X	X		X
Hybrid	X	X	X	X	X
Instructional				X	X
Functional			X		
Sentinel	X	X	X	X	X

As we review this table, we can see that technical SMEs are generally used in analysis and evaluation, since these require the most content-specific resources. Functional

SMEs are most likely only used in the development within a course, and instructional SMEs are going to be used in the implementation and evaluation phases. Hybrid and sentinel SMEs are likely to be useful in all of the ADDIE elements.

If we are able to determine when we will need different types of SMEs, we can accomplish several things at once. First, we will be able to quantify the amount of time each of these experts will need to be plugged into the process. A resource may become overwhelmed if she thinks her time and effort is necessary for the whole design process. This allows us to better define what we ask an individual to contribute, and it allows each individual to gauge the scope of her participation.

Second, we are able to plan our project with a more realistic timeline, plus a resource and cost model that reflects real-world asset allocation. A department head considering whether to allow an SME to work on a project at a 5-10 percent time allocation may be much more likely to participate if he thinks this is not an open-ended commitment with undefined limits.

◇◇◇

Conclusion

As we dig deeper into our relationship with SMEs, we will explore different areas that perhaps you have not thought about or have not experienced in your work. This is a very complex topic, and there has been only a smattering of superficial information and suggestions offered to support the building and maintenance of these important relationships. Starting with knowledge that even the designation of SME can have multiple meanings builds a great foundation for important conversations about our partners in training: the SMEs.

◇◇◇

Discussion Questions

1. How would you define an SME? Do you think there is more than one type of SME?

2. Is it useful for trainers and instructional designers to work with various types of SMEs differently?

3. Do you consider yourself an SME? If so, in what fields?

 ## Case Study Question

You are managing a project that contains several different types of SMEs. It has become obvious that no one has taken the time to identify the types of SMEs the project requires, or has thought about what the differences mean in terms of completing the project successfully.

What do you think is the best way to approach this issue, and what would you do first?

Chapter 2

Selecting Technical SMEs

Chapter Objectives

At the end of chapter 2, you will be able to:

- List at least five SME content-based criteria.
- List at least three SME general skill criteria.
- Produce a rubric for judging and comparing SME criteria.
- Consider nonmeasurable criteria.
- Review several basic SME contract issues.

Chapter Overview

In this chapter, our focus is on the process of rating and selecting technical SMEs, and the various elements of this process that foster success. Choosing the correct TSME assets should be based on an objective system that contains both the necessary criteria and a way to compare each element within both an individual TSME and a group of potential TSMEs. The assessment and selection of any SME will follow these same guidelines, only modified as necessary to cover the required and expected SME skill sets.

Taking the Time to Make Correct SME Selections

The single most important element of starting a project that includes content experts is making sure you are selecting the correct technical SME for your needs. This can be a daunting process, but there are many ways to make selections based on objective criteria. There are several factors that must be considered, and some are only intuitive when you have been involved in selecting and working with this group.

The reason we take this much time and go into this much detail in choosing technical SMEs is because of the reality that if we already had this content knowledge, we wouldn't need the SME. This puts us in the position of making selections based on various factors, usually starting with content knowledge in an area we may know little to nothing about. We need to have some objective way of making these important decisions, or of reviewing choices made by others for us in this environment.

You and the design team may have little or no control over who serves on a committee, and if this ends up being the case, you can at least try to mediate selection based on established criteria for these positions before any final decisions are made. Having objective qualification guidelines might save you from having to work with your CEO's neighbor, who knows almost nothing about almost everything.

Selection Criteria

You should begin by breaking down SME qualifications into two general categories: content-specific and non-content specific. In this way you have both the professional criteria associated with the content itself and the more intangible elements of additional skills that have been found to be important in working with SMEs on training projects.

Content knowledge is much more than just a yes or no. Knowing what to look for in your SMEs has to be based on numerous variables that when combined, offer you a reliable measure of how well a content expert really knows what is important for you in a project. This may seem confusing until you realize the complexity of most content areas. Having general knowledge of a particular content area is far less desirable than having specific content knowledge.

Content-Based Criteria

It comes as no surprise that the first litmus test for any SME is to determine the real level of content knowledge they bring to the project. While generally straightforward and objective, this determination has elements that might not seem obvious or important until you plug in the information and see where your group of content experts actually falls within these key areas.

It is entirely possible that the best known and most recommended content experts don't really fit your needs in a specific area, and you need to know the strengths and weaknesses of each candidate in five areas of content-specificity. These are the key areas you need to review and judge:

- relevance of experience

- depth of experience

- timeliness of experience

- location of experience

- training/teaching experience.

Let's look at these criteria in depth and consider how they affect your committee.

Relevance of Experience

While this may seem like the most obvious and easiest to determine in an SME, reputations and résumés can be deceiving. Many supposed experts with mile-long résumés and spotless reputations may or may not offer much in the way of relevant experience for your project.

First, define relevance for your purposes. Develop a specific list of topics and make sure it is detailed enough to cover each general category of content. If you want to break this down into potential modules or learning elements, it makes your work later much easier. While this will certainly change as you work through the design process, at least you have a valid starting place that allows you a sense of the scope of your requirements.

This gets tricky when you start looking at specific content related to general content requirements. A strong ISD background helps you drill down into the content to see how detailed you really need to be for your specific project needs.

If you are working on a course for customer service reps (CSRs) in a healthcare environment, plans and requirements can be substantially different even within one organization, let alone between providers. "Relevant" in these terms goes beyond healthcare experience and must dig deeper into provider, plan, or organizational relevance.

One person does not fit all requirements when selecting SMEs, and building in time to allow an expert to get up to speed on specific content might be more time than you have to give or budget to cover. Dig down and find out specifically what "relevant" means to you.

Depth of Experience

Just like relevance, depth of experience really matters within your committees. It addresses factors, including time in the field, variety of content-related experience, certification and education related to the content, writing or publishing in the field, and supervisory responsibility related to the content.

When looking at depth, the question you should ask yourself is "How well does this individual really know this specific content?" When you assess SMEs as a group, this becomes somewhat easier, since the comparisons are more obvious between each individual. The tables later in this chapter will help with this process. The challenge is often trying to determine depth in a single SME where there is no real standard for comparison.

While depth of experience might seem like a difference without a distinction when compared to relevant experience, this generally becomes obvious when your content feels generic or is based more on common knowledge than on expert opinion. If content lacks real depth, it is generally because your experts either don't have the necessary depth of experience, or they aren't yet sharing what they know at the level required for your project.

If content lacks real depth, it is generally because your experts either don't have the necessary depth of experience, or they aren't yet sharing what they know at the level required for your project.

Since you aren't an expert in most content areas, you have to rely on your instincts, and the knowledge you do have to make this determination. Your non-technical SME groups can be very valuable in helping you through the maze.

Timeliness of Experience

The timeliness of an expert's experience is the third factor in the selection process. The time and type of his most recent experience can be critical in determining his suitability to serve as an SME. Some professional course designers won't seriously consider any SME that has more than a one-year gap in direct hands-on experience with the content.

One factor in determining your qualifications is the shelf life of the content you are working with. Well-established and stable content that only changes incrementally over time is less affected than state-of-the-art content that may change on an hourly basis. Also consider that some content areas are only marginally influenced by time, and the changes that do exist are more in products than in techniques. Many times, this is the case in the skilled trades of technical training, where changing a specific product only affects one minor variable in a much larger process. Using a newer type of mortar when laying a line of brick is not as critical a difference as between laying brick and laying block.

On the other end of the scale, technology tends to have a shelf life measured in minutes. Do you really want an SME who has expert credentials only in version 2.0 of a software package when you are working on a training program for version 3?

Location of Experience

Thinking about geography when selecting SMEs might seem puzzling, until you consider that even minute changes in location can have an impact on content. Depending on your project, failing to account for the location of an expert's experience can either marginally or completely affect your work. Let's look at several examples.

If you are working on a project to train paramedics that has a regional or national scope, each jurisdiction potentially has different skill requirements, licensure requirements, and clinical requirements for participants. Some may require 180 hours in clinical practice and some may require 80. This is a huge difference in terms of designing training. Knowledge of these differing standards is critical.

When designing technical and skills training, geographic location can be a critical element. The elements of geography that affect content include weather variables like temperature ranges and humidity; soil and ground condition variables like clay versus sand; and earthquake, hurricane, flood, and other natural disaster potential. To an outsider looking in, these variables may seem minor at best or even unimportant, but nothing could be further from the truth. A content expert who has only worked in a warm climate has no relevant information for cold climate situations, and building codes are certainly different in quake-prone areas compared to others with little, if any, quake activity. These are just examples, but depending on your situation, there could be many differences that you need to represent on your committee.

The other regional variation that often comes to the surface in SME committees is jargon. This not only applies to tools and equipment, it also comes up in the names of processes and procedures that are exactly the same, but called one thing in California and another in Connecticut. This can be a major problem down the line if it isn't addressed early in the process. You can't have a large percentage of your end-user population trying to figure out your terminology because you didn't allow for regional variations in your SME group.

One indirect consideration here is that a budget may not allow for the cost of bringing in dispersed committee members. You may have to choose members who can represent the locational variations within the committee, or use remote conferencing options.

Training/Teaching Experience

If you are working on a project that has a training deliverable (and how many don't?), having an SME with training experience can be a valuable asset to the process. Knowing what works and doesn't work during implementation can be a critical added dimension. Many times, it is this SME who eventually teaches the content, and having the connection at this stage of the process may lessen the disconnect issues from the design to implementation stages.

It will be useful to determine if the training and teaching experiences are relevant to the content and eventual implementation choices. A career as a classroom teacher may not work to your benefit if you are designing online learning using a learning management system (LMS), since the approaches are so different.

The same is true for the level of teaching experience. Teachers working in higher education generally don't connect with workplace learning in the same way an apprenticeship instructor would.

The possible downside to having training experience in an SME is the second-guessing of some decisions and approaches based on an expert's opinion about what has worked best for them over the years, which may or may not have any relevance to your work.

If you want to use a scoring system for these qualifications, Table 2-1 shows one way to document each criteria using a 0–3 scale. You can change this to any scale that works best for your situation. This example includes fictional initials in the left column, plus some sample scores so you can see how this might look in practice.

Table 2-1: Scoring Content-Based Criteria

Name	Relevance	Depth	Timeliness	Location	T/T Exp.	Total
WEF	1	1	3	3	1	9
MRT	2	3	2	1	3	11
SAR	3	3	3	2	3	14

Scale is 0 to 3 with 0 designating no qualifications, 1 designating a minimum qualification, 2 designating an average qualification, and 3 designating highly qualified. NA designates no relevance for this project.

General Skills Criteria

After you have worked through the critical issues of SME content-based criteria, you still have to consider a content expert's skills that directly affect the workflow process in your project. Even the best and brightest might not be a workable fit for your needs. These often neglected variables can be rather easily gauged, and you might even harvest some pleasant surprises within your group.

The most important general skills criteria to consider include:

- communication ability
- writing ability
- sociability.

Communication Ability

This may seem obvious, but having an expert who can communicate with you and the other committee members is nothing short of critical in some situations. And think of communication in several different ways. We all have experience with experts who obviously know the content but are unable to efficiently and effectively communicate necessary information when it comes to working with the committee. On the other hand, overly verbal experts can drown the content in minutiae and slow things to a crawl.

The overly patronizing individual can alienate everyone—even other content experts—and should be avoided if viable options on other criteria exist. Some individuals also refuse to explain or modify jargon in environments where it isn't necessary.

While this is admittedly subjective criteria, it is not to be dismissed out of hand. Together with sociability, which we discuss later in this chapter, these two criteria are the often ignored momentum stoppers that can have unintended results.

Writing Ability

A real plus in a committee member is the ability to write content-related supplemental materials. There are times when an expert can more effectively reduce a process to writing than a team of instructional designers or technical writers. Even the ability to sketch out an outline can save hours and days in writing.

How someone writes is also a consideration, since many academic and technical SMEs write in very academic and technical styles, which may not be appropriate for your work. It is sometimes more work rewriting their submissions than just not having them contribute at all, since the translation from formal to less formal styles is not easy for some.

I have seen several cases where SMEs were hired with the idea that they would create case studies or design role-play scenarios, and their writing was so poor the trainers needed to hire a writer as well as pay the SME. There are variations on this theme relating to report writing and other mundane project requirements that SMEs are commonly expected to contribute.

Be mindful of possible roadblocks concerning language. There are some SMEs who do not have English as a first language, and while valuable contributors on the content side, may not be able to produce written documents in English at your desired level of proficiency. This also applies to English-speaking SMEs contributing to a project that will be offered in Spanish, French, or another language.

While it may not be expected that an SME is a good writer or can pull research together for the project, the occasional content expert who enjoys doing this work can make your project more efficient, and usually increases the quality of the product. If at some point you can determine who likes to write and is actually pretty good at it, you may find a resource that is worth the effort to encourage and to integrate into the team.

Sociability

While this criterion is subjective at best, there is nothing that closes down an SME committee faster than one or more members who don't make an effort to get along and work as a team member. The reasons for this are as varied as each individual, but if you evaluate members' sense of sociability when choosing, you won't have to remove or replace members during the process. Better to choose on the basis of caution if possible. However, there are some indispensable experts you just have to live with.

Professionals with a reputation for being difficult, arrogant, patronizing, self-promoting, or elitist can grind a project to a halt until they are removed or involved in an attitude-readjustment meeting or two.

Table 2-2: Scoring General Criteria

Name	Com Ability	Writing	Sociability	Total
WEF	3	2	3	8
MRT	1	2	1	4
SAR	3	2	3	8

Scale is 0 to 3 with 0 designating no qualifications, 1 designating a minimum qualification, 2 designating an average qualification, and 3 designating highly qualified. NA designates no relevance for this project.

Putting It All Together

Now that you have the basics of how you want to review the qualifications of potential SMEs, let's collect all of the criteria in one place and create a form that allows you to painlessly gather data and make decisions.

Table 2-3: Combined Scoring Criteria

Name:	Content-Based Rating	General Rating	Total Rating
WEF	9	8	17
MRT	11	4	15
SAR	14	8	22

Let's assume that we now have a candidate to evaluate and we begin to enter our ratings based on the information we have available:

Table 2-4: Comparing Specific SME Ratings for General and Content-Based Criteria

	Name: WEF	Name: MRT	Name:	Name:
Relevance	1	2		
Depth	1	3		
Timeliness	3	2		
Location	3	1		
T/T Experience	1	3		
Communication	3	1		
Writing	2	2		
Sociability	3	1		
Total	17	15		
Average	2.125	1.875		

Scale is 0 to 3 with 0 designating no qualifications, 1 designating a minimum qualification, 2 designating an average qualification, and 3 designating highly qualified. NA designates no relevance for this project.

Based on this review, you have two candidates with similar average qualifications. Let's compare that to a much more qualified candidate.

Table 2-5: Comparing Candidates

	Name: WEF	Name: MRT	Name: SAR	Name:
Relevance	1	2	3	
Depth	1	3	3	
Timeliness	3	2	3	
Location	3	1	2	
T/T Experience	1	3	3	
Communication	3	1	3	
Writing	2	2	2	
Sociability	3	1	3	
Total	17	15	22	
Average	2.125	1.875	2.75	

Scale is 0 to 3 with 0 designating no qualifications, 1 designating a minimum qualification, 2 designating an average qualification, and 3 designating highly qualified. NA designates no relevance for this project.

Based on this largely objective review, candidate SAR is much more qualified to be your SME on this project than candidate MRT. But as with all such reviews, they are only a place to start your comparisons.

As you begin to work with these forms and grading criteria, you will find there are probably elements you want to add or subtract to fit your needs. You can also change the rating scales and all of the variables to produce a format that works for you. These are only suggestions to get started.

Nonmeasurable Criteria to Review and Consider

There are certain aspects of this selection process that are not well served by charting and assigning value, since they are more important when looking at the group you choose more than just an individual. In these categories, you need to look at the balance to make sure you have made choices that work well together.

Organizational Standing

This is a nice way of saying that you need to be sensitive to the mix of managers, engineers, craftspeople, and other distinct types of members in your committee. When this mix is out of kilter, role perceptions and posturing may impede your committee productivity. You don't want to potentially silence any of your SMEs based on the perceived—or perhaps real—threat that participation might have repercussions beyond the safe environment of the project.

There is no right or wrong in this chemistry, but there should be some consideration of how it all works together. Having one or more of your experts feeling cornered or demeaned can kill any forward motion. You also don't want one or more of your group not willing to be forthcoming because a manager or other supervisor may not agree or appreciate their point of view.

There is always the potential to have non-process issues affect a committee, and some of it is unavoidable. The most likely scenarios deal with non-content personality and posturing issues between individual committee members. In extreme situations, it may be necessary to revise your committee membership as needed. It is also possible to have SMEs work more independently and have their work incorporated into the process without acting as a committee in the traditional sense.

Managing the SME Contract

Once decisions are made about who is going to participate, the process of making sure everyone is on the same page begins. This isn't just related to paid SMEs or consultants, this relates to everyone who is going to be part of the SME group. Many times the internal SMEs require more negotiating than the external participants because of time and budget implications.

Contracts exist with your SMEs regardless of whether they are formal legal documents (beyond the scope of this discussion) or informal verbal agreements related to every aspect of the process. No matter what you decide, make sure it is all written, and discussed and modified as necessary. Experience proves that taking this step early will save you countless headaches later. Even the most minor misinterpretation or variable left unresolved can turn up as an issue later on either side of the relationship.

While each situation is different and the variables involved are limitless, there is a short list of issues that almost always crop up during these pre-participation discussions. The time to come to agreements on these is before you get started, or you may spend twice the time fixing the problems later with everyone under a different set of assumptions.

Available and Committed Time

Making sure you have a firm grasp of how much time each SME has agreed to commit to your project is the first step in managing your resources. You will need to negotiate both how much time will be allocated and when the time will be made available to you. Both of these are equally important, but you may find that getting SME time when you need it is more difficult than agreeing to how much time will be involved.

Estimating total time commitments can be a challenge that experience will eventually make more obvious. The variables to consider include the type of work the SME will be providing, travel time, deliverables required, time that involves working with others, and more.

In some cases, a time and materials approach (only paying for what you actually need), will work to your advantage if you don't have a firm grasp of how much time will really be needed. In other cases, setting a total of committed hours will help you budget. Always be cautious of scope creep, which might involve hearing from an SME that your requested deliverable is much more detailed and involved than originally thought, and more time is needed to complete the work. If this is a concern, negotiate SME time by deliverable rather than by an hourly rate.

The bigger issue for internal SME loans is usually when the content expert will be available and for how long.

Internal SME time commitment can be a complicated process, since personnel and HR policy are often involved and detailed cost-center or budget allocations must be negotiated and resolved.

The bigger issue for internal SME loans is usually when the content expert will be available and for how long. Let's say you negotiate 80 hours of SME time in the next year with a supervisor in another department. If you don't specify when those 80 hours are going to be made available to you, it may end up that you have the last two weeks of the budget year open to you, which are probably close to useless in your project planning. Make sure you have the correct weekly or daily allocation of hours stipulated in your agreement so you can plan accordingly. Waiting for an SME to be released on a key aspect of your project is less than enjoyable.

How Long Is a Day?

Negotiating SME commitments can involve some very interesting interpretations of what a specific length of time means to everyone involved. This same issue includes every aspect of your budget. Being ahead of this discussion can save your project later. Even the basics like "How long is a day?" will creep into this at one point or another.

First ask yourself, "What is a day?" in your project plan. In some organizations, a day is defined as a set number of hours of direct involvement in the work process. In others, a day might mean simply being available to assist. I have seen some organizations consider one minute worked on a project in a calendar day as a one-day billing entry.

An SME consultant might generally charge a minimum for any contact with your project. It is not uncommon for a phone call or conference call to be billed at a minimum of one, two, or four hours and any travel time—locally or longer—is charged from port-to-port in four-hour increments. So, a five-hour trip is billed as eight hours of time. I don't have any value judgment for the way anyone charges for their time, since many busy SMEs can easily command any reasonable rate they choose to bill. My point is that if you don't have this information before you get started, your first billing invoice might shock you.

Make sure you have all hourly, incremental, travel, per diem, parking, lodging, communication, copying, standby, meeting, conference, and other time- and cost-based variables discussed and agreed to before you start. This is just as important with internal SME loans, too, since copy costs, travel, overtime, and other miscellaneous expenses might be considered your responsibility even if the individuals are on loan. The "one big family" organizational philosophy may end at the departmental budget line.

◇◇

Conclusion

When selecting any technical SME resource, make sure you perform due diligence and know what you are getting. Making tough decisions at the beginning of the selection process is much easier than changing decisions later, and a certain set of expectations exist already.

If you have little or no control over the selection process, at least attempt to include some level of objective selection criteria into the discussion for those making these decisions. Even if this process is completely political and based more on personality than résumé, you at least have a reference point later to suggest changes based on any content experts not living up to required levels of participation or knowledge.

At all times, scan the horizon for positive and negative issues that may affect your project. Just as often, we are surprised by the quality and performance of an SME, as we are disappointed in what we were sure was a valuable resource.

Discussion Questions

1. What do you think is the single most important content-based criterion for selecting an SME?

2. Do you think there are times when you can overthink the selection process, and you might be better off just finding someone who is easy to work with on projects?

3. Is there any single criterion that would keep you from selecting an otherwise-qualified SME?

 ## Case Study Question

You are just beginning an important curriculum design project, and you will need a small committee of SMEs to work with you to suggest content and skills. You have been told that the SME appointments have already been made, and you have no choice in the selections, since the group is coming from an engineering department that has just been declared redundant and needs to have staff reassigned. You have no idea if any of them are qualified to work on your content. What do you do in this situation? Do you have any alternatives?

Chapter 3

TSME Committee Structure

Chapter Objectives

At the end of chapter 3, you will be able to:

- Describe three possible SME committee structures.
- List ways to both find and support TSME leadership.
- Describe a basic support structure for TSME committees.
- Describe several ways to conduct pilot testing with SMEs.

Chapter Overview

The process of forming and supporting your SME committees is a critical element in your project. Taking time to do this correctly sets the foundation for everything else you do with this group of professionals. These first impressions and victories can last for years, and span many future projects.

SMEs perform countless different functions in limitless environments. In each case, there are unique circumstances and demands that forge different relationships between content experts and their organizational contacts. From my experience, the utilization of TSMEs has a pattern that falls into several well-defined structures for their integration into the design function.

Everything covered on this topic also applies to HSMEs as well as TSMEs, depending on the circumstances and how you decide to work with your SMEs.

While there are many TSMEs who work independently with designers and trainers, large-scale projects often have at least one committee of content experts, or multiple committees depending on the scope of the project. Having a plan for how to structure these varying SME needs will always work to your benefit.

Don't be too worried about scaling up a project to include more TSMEs and more committees, since the challenges are not any greater, except in scale between one committee and 10 committees working at the same time. In fact, there are some advantages derived from having larger-scale committee structures. Each set of circumstances is different, but keep an open mind about choices in this regard.

TSME Committee Structures

It is impossible to overemphasize the importance of building effective and productive SME committees in any project where they are involved. Having a strategy of simply finding a place at the table for your content experts rarely works as well as having a plan in place to both choose and nurture your SMEs.

One of the most daunting tasks an instructional designer faces is building and managing these committees. Whether they are formed to gather practices and procedures for an apprenticeship program, analyze the steps necessary to install and maintain sophisticated technical systems, or assemble a skill-building program in leadership, these SME groups are the nucleus around which you build your content.

This process is always more complicated than just gathering the content. Managing SME committees requires a skill set that includes (at a minimum): diplomacy, project management, and leadership. How to structure and support your committees are always going to be questions that have to be answered.

Finding a way to make a committee work efficiently and effectively is not a matter of chance—it requires a plan and making sure these committees are managed and respected as more than just a gathering of experts. These are actually micro-cultures with distinctive personalities and characteristics.

In some ways, working with SME committees is similar to working with any other committee. But assuming that normal approaches to this process will always work may not always be effective. The biggest mistake trainers make in working with SME committees is not taking the time and energy to manage this process just like any other element of course design.

Case Study: Consolidating Diverse SME Committees

A very large multinational training organization had recently decided to consolidate numerous diverse SME curriculum development teams that had never worked together before under the leadership of a single training function. Every course these teams developed looked different and there was no standardization in the way the courses were designed. Some didn't even contain objectives or evaluations. The organization wanted to create courses that were designed using ISD and had a consistent look and feel regardless of the originating SME committee. They also expected this would be a more cost-effective way to design curriculum and to minimize duplication of efforts among the curriculum design groups. For example, each group had a basic safety course that was almost identical to what the other committees designed. The largest challenges to this approach were getting SME buy-in to these changes and standardizing the design process. There were a total of five different SME committees that had never worked together or designed curriculum the same way.

The organization worked with a university-based ISD group to establish one curriculum design function, including a project director and one instructional designer assigned to each SME committee. Each SME committee had an appointed chair to work with the project director and instructional designers. A materials development function was created to assist all of the SME committees in creating one look and feel for all courses. Additionally, all of the committees were brought together for an initial group of meetings that included background on the ISD process and training on a standard method for each SME committee to use to design courses. The SME committees met four times a year in person, with all groups in attendance, and work was shared among committees and the design team between meetings.

The process and approach worked so well that the number of SME committees eventually doubled, and the organization eventually brought all of the course design work in-house to further control costs.

Scale

There are times when the scale of SME involvement just doesn't allow for anything less than a complete strategy for making this element of your project work at high efficiency. You might be able to wing it with one or two content experts, but working with 30 or more at once demands a plan. Let's take a look at both extremes.

At one end of the spectrum, working with SMEs might involve incorporating one or two SMEs on a project. This may be a very informal relationship and may only require a minimal investment in building and sustaining a long-term relationship with each SME. They are typically treated as "one and done," and instructional designers put little thought into much more than gathering the necessary content information and moving on to the next challenge.

The other extreme is the large project and large SME-group integration that includes numerous instructional designers, SMEs, and support staff. These very complex and demanding team structures can range from two or three SMEs forming one committee, to 30 or more SMEs working on subcommittees concentrating on various individual content areas. From my experience, I have had projects with 10 or more SME committees consisting of five or more SMEs working at the same time in the same location. Each committee worked with a different instructional designer, and support staff was available for copying and other associated on-site tasks.

No matter where you fall on the continuum of small to extremely large, the basics of the process are pretty much the same, with scale being the one variable.

Getting Started

Regardless of the scale, paying attention to several basic elements of committee formation and operation will always work in your favor. The important elements you need to pay attention to at the start of the process are

- committee structure
- selecting leadership
- building the support environment.

There will always be other variables involved, like organizational culture issues, personalities, securing release time for SMEs, and the always-popular budget and deadline headaches, but getting your committee started on firm ground allows time to deal with other inevitable issues that arise on every project. We will discuss those inevitable issues later in the book.

Committee Structures

Once you have a good handle on your committee members, it's time to think about how you want to structure your committee. There will be some influence on your structure choices based on the committee members. It is also possible location and availability will affect your structure. In all cases, there are several different ways to go.

Table 3-1: Committee Structures

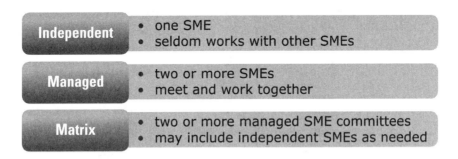

Independent	• one SME • seldom works with other SMEs
Managed	• two or more SMEs • meet and work together
Matrix	• two or more managed SME committees • may include independent SMEs as needed

Independent Committee

In this structure, committee members work independently for all or most of their time as an SME—with direction from the training group. This structure works best for small discreet assignments that don't involve or require more than one content expert working at a time on a particular content issue. There is usually no reason for SMEs to gather or work together as a group in this structure.

Table 3-2: An SME and the Design Function

Managed Committee

When you have a lot of material to cover, two or more SMEs working together, and more than one meeting of an SME committee is required, it is usually most productive to have a managed committee structure. Managed committees consist of an instructional designer and two or more content experts who gather together to work on a project. This group will meet together on as many occasions as required to get the work completed. Meetings may be in person or may have members participate remotely.

Table 3-3: A Group of SMEs and the Design Function

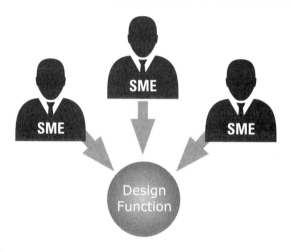

Matrix Committee

When working on really large projects with several SME committees and design staff, using a matrix committee structure allows for the flexibility necessary to move and scale resources as needed during the project. Matrix committees include both independent and managed committees created and closed as the workload requires. The committees are connected to a central design function that both manages and supports the committee's work with the content. Instead of having resources assigned to each individual committee, they are available and dispersed as needed and requested.

Table 3-4: SME Committees and the Design Function

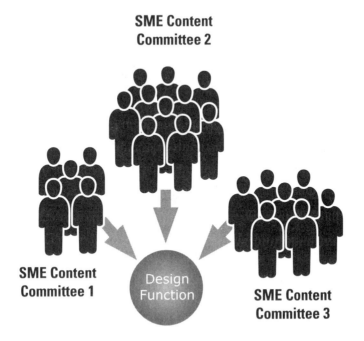

SME Content
Committee 2

SME Content
Committee 1

Design
Function

SME Content
Committee 3

Range-of-Experience TSME Committee

I have seen several SME committees with content experts who were selected based on their range of experience, not on the depth, relevance, and recency of their experience. Different levels of content experience balances out the problem of any experienced SMEs who are not able to talk about the content at a level that the audience will understand. For example, engineers in computer science who serve as SMEs are sometimes not able to relate effectively to a population of students who are going to use a new software package for the first time.

The most effective way to initiate this approach is to have three levels of content experts on your committee:

- New SME – 1-3 years of direct experience with the content
- Middle SME – 3-10 years of direct experience with the content
- Senior SME – 10 or more years of direct recent experience with the content.

Table 3-5: SME Range of Experience

New and middle SMEs are much more likely to ask for and provide detail in areas that senior SMEs take for granted. This also applies to documenting steps in a process and sequencing steps for the repair or maintenance of equipment. Senior SMEs have a tendency to make assumptions about what others should know—both other SMEs and the end users of a project. This may cause very large gaps in critical details about a process, skill, or other knowledge necessary for the content to be taught.

In the apprenticeship SME committees, it is sometimes the case that an apprentice or journey worker will join the SME group at different times to offer opinions and suggestions from the end-user perspective. These sessions can be really valuable in making sure the learner is represented, which helps eliminate problems before implementation.

You can have as many of each of these as desired to get your best mix of experience levels. Sometimes the instructional designer can serve the new SME function, since she will probably not have much experience in the content and will ask the follow-up questions to assist this process.

Committee Size

It is important that you have a well-reasoned number of SMEs working together in a managed committee. Too many participants and you may have a hard-to-manage group. Too small a committee and you may risk having too little content knowledge represented. Besides, committee work might be too much to divide among a small group.

Groups in the range of three to five content experts usually work best. This of course depends on many factors, but my experience has shown that many more than this leads to at least one or two idle members who don't seem to have any real obligation to the group, and only marginally participate. This is also a very manageable size for discussions and work assignments. I also like to have an odd number on these committees to avoid stalemates on decisions the group needs to make.

Table 3-6: Additional Committee Considerations

Consideration:	Benefits:
SME leadership	• Stability and efficiency. • Start meetings on time and stay on track. • Keep everyone on task and engaged. • Better with an insider than an outsider.
ISD support	• Efficient process flow. • Keeps questions, problems, and other issues within easy facilitation. • Keeps everyone aware of project priorities. • Keeps design or project information as the first priority. • Builds a process/relationship foundation for future projects.
Administrative support	• Ensures the SMEs have everything they need. • Enables the designer to turn the rough content data into objectives and evaluation tasks without having to interpret notes.
Pilot testing	• Any content-related issues that come up in pilot testing can be most easily addressed by the SMEs when they are involved. • They can deal with missing content, too much or too little content for the implementation time allocated, or too complex or too simple content. • SMEs have an opportunity to observe what their content looks like in the final training product. • This can be a real milestone in the development of SME assets for the training function in the future.

Selecting and Supporting SME Leadership

Regardless of the committee members and structure you choose for a project, the ability to recognize and support leadership within the SME groups helps support stability and efficiency. You want to have an SME as chair for each managed committee to handle the basic operational functions of the group while you have meetings. You need to have meetings start on time and stay on track, and the more the SMEs can do this for themselves, the better it will go.

Your SME leadership will also be especially valuable when the committees are not together, but are working on documents and projects between meetings. You need to have someone keeping everyone on task and engaged, and this goes much better if done by a committee member and not by the training staff.

Instructional Design Support

The most efficient SME committees are those that have an instructional designer assigned to work with the group. Depending on the structure of the group, the ISD might also be the chair, either officially or unofficially. In either case, having a design professional with your content group allows a very efficient process flow and keeps questions, problems, and other associated issues within easy facilitation. Committees can sometimes be unguided missiles if left to function alone, since they might not have the design or project information as their first priority, or even have knowledge of it.

Also, building a working relationship between the design and content expert committee members builds a foundation for whatever work will likely follow on other projects. Later work will simply be an extension of the original relationship, with the difference being the content and product—not the process. This alone can be a major time and resources savings.

Building a working relationship between the design and content expert committee members builds a foundation for whatever work will likely follow on other projects.

Building the Support Environment

Making sure your content experts have the resources they need makes a big difference in success for your committees. Sometimes it is as simple as making copies or getting a file printed. Other times it might be a bit more complicated, like having someone take notes and keep track of changes and versions of documents. In all cases, be ready before the request and have the necessary support available.

Make sure a design professional is also at hand to turn the rough content data into objectives and evaluation tasks without having to interpret notes or guess at the will of the group concerning key content issues. The immediacy of this interaction saves large amounts of time and trouble as the project builds and the deliverables are assembled.

Pilot Testing and SMEs

The most often ignored and under-budgeted aspect of instructional design—after analysis—is pilot testing. In most situations the functional pilot-testing phase is actually implementation itself, and it doesn't take a seasoned trainer to figure out the risks of this approach.

While the general subject of pilot testing is beyond the scope of this book, the role SMEs play in this process is inherently linked to the way you facilitate this aspect of your projects. You can review *ISD From the Ground Up* or other ASTD publications for ideas on the best way to pilot. SMEs are the link between the design and the implementation of your courses, and including them in all aspects of the course design will enhance the value of your product.

SMEs are the link between the design and the implementation of your courses, and including them in all aspects of the course design will enhance the value of your product.

There are several important aspects to this process that warrant the integration of some or all of your SME groups. The most obvious reason to integrate SMEs into pilot testing is that they are the source of the content, and any content-related issues that come up in pilot testing can be most easily addressed by the SMEs. These will often fall into the categories of missing content, too much or too little content for the implementation time allocated, or content that is either too complex or too simple for the target population.

As the pilot testing runs its course, any of these issues can be discussed and addressed by the SMEs and design team. If you have an HSME implementing the pilot course, you have the additional asset of having a trainer's viewpoint on what to correct.

The other less obvious but equally important reason to have SMEs involved in the pilot is that they have an opportunity to observe what their content looks like in the final training product. The value of this exposure to the real world of training during implementation is an eye-opener for the uninitiated SME. It will influence the way they think about content the next time they are involved in a project. It may also create an interest in being a facilitator or taking on a larger role in future course development projects.

One other excellent idea in situations where you have more than one organization or different locations participating in a project is to have someone from one organization participate in the pilot in another organization. The effects of this are almost too good to be true in both team building and evaluation of the product. If you can possibly do this in any situation, take advantage of the opportunity.

If at all practical, include your SMEs in the pilot-testing process and watch and listen as they offer their perspectives on what they observe. This is a real milestone in the development of SME assets for the training function in the future.

◇◇◇

Conclusion

Making sure you design your SME committees to their best advantage is not as difficult as it might appear in the beginning. Taking time in the beginning to think this through opens many positive opportunities for success for this and all future projects with these SMEs.

◇◇◇

Discussion Questions

1. Do you think it is a good idea to have SME committee chairs or leadership within the SMEs? Are there times when it isn't a good idea?

2. Is it possible to have too large an SME committee working on a project? How about too small a committee or only one SME? How do you know the correct number of SMEs to use?

3. Is using SMEs as observers a good idea when pilot testing a new course?

 Case Study Question

You are managing a very large design project, and you presently have five SME committees working on different aspects of the course at the same time. You think the process is going very well but there is some concern over the cost of having committees working at the same time at the same place. What do you say to those that think there is a less expensive way to accomplish the same results?

Chapter 4

Welcoming SMEs to the Process

Chapter Objectives

At the end of chapter 4, you will be able to:

- Describe the differences between design cultures and SME cultures.
- List several ways to ensure you make a positive first impression with SMEs.
- Define at least one formula for successful starts with SMEs.
- List the roles and responsibilities for every SME working on a project.
- Describe the most effective kickoff meeting for your needs.

Chapter Overview

You should always welcome new SMEs to the process of instructional design. Ensure they know how much they are appreciated and how important they are to the process of curriculum design.

Getting Started

You can never overstate the importance of beginning a cooperative project with SMEs in a way that is both welcoming and informative. Not only does it create a positive working environment, it also telegraphs how you approach the design process—and ultimately how everyone will be treated. When it comes to creating a successful working relationship, organized and honest trumps "business as usual" in almost every scenario.

Remember that your new SMEs are generally unfamiliar with the workflow, process dynamics, and priorities that a project team lives and breathes every day. An important first step is to make sure that everyone discusses and agrees to process guidelines, ground rules, deadlines, and other essential task-related elements. It is sometimes a revelation to SMEs that these even exist in this process, and the rigor and complexity of these projects are not always visible or appreciated from the outside looking in.

While it may seem obvious, outreach to the SME family in your work needs to be sincere, welcoming, informative, and professional. One of the biggest mistakes designers make early in the process of working with SMEs is to appear patronizing and impatient. This attitude can quickly become a hurdle that is never fully bridged, and may actually doom a project to mediocrity when SMEs only participate at a minimal level, when they have so much more to offer. It can also lead to passive-aggressive behaviors like failing to proofread documents or providing minimal input in key areas. A very few may actually want a project to fail to prove a point about who is more important in the process.

Design Culture vs. the SME Culture

While content experts work in every conceivable environment, it is fair to say that few if any of them will have worked on a training project before, unless they were on a previous SME committee or project. Therefore there is a cultural difference. While most of the experts likely feel positive about the process of designing curriculum, there are some who need attention and care to ensure they feel welcome and involved.

Making the First Impression

The first obvious difference is to be mindful of the fact that some SMEs may not have much experience in an office environment. I remember one of my first adventures as an SME in the telephone industry, and I went directly from climbing poles to sitting in a really nice office with trainers who were smartly dressed and at complete ease in this environment. I had on dirty jeans and a t-shirt accompanied by battered climbing boots. To say I was uncomfortable was an understatement.

I was very fortunate the training group I was working with was welcoming and completely indifferent to my dress. They noticed my obvious "fish out of water" feeling of discomfort and responded with warmth. As a result, my initial SME role turned into an incredible customer service program and course that planted the seed for me wanting to be a trainer and later, a designer. Their bright smiles and offers of coffee turned an awkward moment into a life-changing professional experience, and I have always reflected on that time and place when I have worked with others in my role as a designer and trainer.

I recently had an experience where an SSME was given an invitation to attend a project team's casual dinner that has become a tradition on this project. In attendance from around the country were 10 or so TSMEs, five instructional designers, and several support staff. We were very pleased when our SSME arrived with his wife and joined us for a very casual dinner together. During the dinner we learned that it was his birthday and also the anniversary of his first date with his wife. He was so invested in this project and felt so attached to us as a team member that he drove nearly 80 miles round-trip and shared his birthday and anniversary with us because he felt like family and didn't want to miss this celebration of our working together. Another of many examples of how important it is to welcome and encourage all SMEs to be part of the family in your projects.

There are as many variations on these experiences as there are SMEs and trainers, and hopefully most of them turn out the same. It will require extra effort from the design team to see that this initial experience grows into something more permanent, even if it is just the goodwill that training offers the SME community.

Case Study: Creating an SME-Friendly Course Development Process

A consortium of six organizations from different parts of the country decided to join resources with a training organization to create a series of courses for a specific maintenance function that is common to all the organizations. In the past, each partner had either designed their own courses, paid to have them designed, or in many cases, had no courses in specific areas. They all felt that splitting the cost six ways would certainly save money and resources for everyone while also producing a complete training package with a national focus and credibility.

A system was set up that required one management and one labor representative to participate as TSMEs from each organization in the course design process. These technical committees would work on specific courses with the assistance of instructional designers. Very few of these SMEs had ever worked on a course design process before this project.

From the very beginning, the focus of this project was to make the SMEs the center of all project activity to ensure both the best content and the best working relationship. SMEs were involved in all decisions relating to project operations, like meeting locations and times, as well as product decisions such as choosing the format for the training modules. Each specific SME committee working on a course also chose co-chairs to help facilitate discussion and to work directly with the project design team.

One important aspect of the SME relationship that was taken very seriously was communicating with the SMEs on a regular basis, not just on content-specific information, but also concerning the project. The other key to the success of this project was celebrating each milestone in the project. Every time a course was completed and taken through pilot testing, a celebration was held at the next meeting of the SMEs. Major milestones like completing a whole series of courses were celebrated with a dinner for all of the SMEs and instructional designers. At these events, everyone was encouraged to say how they felt about the project and working with the team. To the surprise of many, everyone had something positive to say, and some of the quietest SMEs were the ones that had the most to say in support of the project.

In-House Operational Differences

Another cultural difference that can occur when in-house SMEs join the training function is professional structure and rigidity. A group of engineers will likely have a completely different professional culture than the training group. Attorneys and medical professionals are also used to a certain work environment. In fact, just about any SME will be at least in a moderately different organizational space, even if you work for the same organization.

This is sometimes benign and involves issues like work hours and lunch arrangements, and it can also involve more substantive differences like locations of meetings and staff support. The expectations of either side of this partnership might need to be a little more flexible than usual, and everyone should accept that somewhere in the middle works best for all.

Outside SMEs

The world of consulting SMEs is huge, and the way they are welcomed to the family really makes a difference to both their support of your project and the chances of you working with them in the future. You will be compared to the best experiences they have as an SME, and you want to be at the top of their list for multiple reasons.

While all new SMEs should be afforded the best treatment as they begin, you will notice that this consulting group has a different set of expectations. The general theme of the more experienced consulting content experts is a desire to work quickly and efficiently, with a minimum of time-wasting frustrations, such as trying to find contact information, or knowing where to forward invoices and travel requests. There is more of a business-first attitude with this group, and they like to cut to the chase when it comes to process. They expect to be treated the same way you expect to be treated, and the relationship thrives when everyone keeps this in mind.

Formula for Successful Starts

Having a great plan for your SMEs is just as important as any other aspect of your project. A winning formula includes several elements that can be modified to meet your specific situation:

- first outreach
- contact and communication information
- SME roles and responsibilities
- project details
- background materials
- kickoff meeting.

Table 4-1: Formula for Successful Starts

First Outreach	Project Details
• Be welcome and informative. • Be quick and thorough. • Include the project name and formal descriptions. • Clear up misinformation.	• Share any information about timelines, deadlines, and deliverables. • Share any relevant elements of a project management plan that includes key dates and deliverables. • Provide an organizational chart that lists key personnel and their role in the organization.
Contact and Communication Information	**Background Materials**
• Provide accurate contact information. • Provide your plan for communication. • Include all forms of contact: phone, email, group file-access portals, webinars, conferencing. • Give username and password info for: voicemail access, file-sharing, web- and phone-based accounts.	• This varies for each project, but can be grant proposals, existing courses and content information, outside consulting work and reports, accreditation reports, and internal reports on training gaps. • Include information on ISD and the ADDIE model.
SME Roles and Responsibilities	**Kickoff Meeting**
• Share some basic structural overviews. • Clarify misconceptions. • Generate any questions that need to be addressed. • Explain the role of the SME in your project. • Provide a brief overview of your role in the process. • You may share an overview of each individual's role in the team.	• Align everyone with the same information and expectations. • Time for formal welcome and providing particulars. • Time to clear up any possibly negative elements of the project. • Give introductions, clarify responsibilities, and resolve housekeeping issues. • Introduce a set of ground rules the group will follow during the project.

First Outreach

The initial contact with your SMEs should be immediately after assignments are confirmed and you know for sure that someone is onboard. You should be both welcoming and informative, and this should be in writing either by email or more formally if appropriate. Regardless of the vehicle, you need to be quick and thorough with this first communication.

The project name and other formal descriptions should be included in case there is any confusion or there has been a lack of information up to this point. It is not unheard of for an SME to be assigned to a project with little if any information about what they will be doing. It is also possible that someone may have a different understanding about the project content or scope, and your outreach is the first solid piece of information they have received. It is much better to clear up any misinformation before you get started.

Contact and Communication Information

One of the first things you want to distribute to your SME group is accurate contact information and your plan for communicating with the group. The contact information needs to include all reasonable forms of contact, including phone, email, and any group file-access portals. If you have already determined whether to use webinars or other forms of conferencing, make this information available.

One often forgotten element of this process is to make sure that everyone has username and password information for new accounts they may need to use. This can include voicemail access, file-sharing functions, and web- and phone-based accounts you will use. If you don't yet have accounts established or have access information, at least let everyone know this is coming up and that you will forward that information to them.

SME Roles and Responsibilities

There is often a fair amount of confusion about expectations among SMEs first starting a project. Some of this comes from past experiences—good and bad—and some exists because this is a new responsibility with no prior knowledge of how things will work. While a more formal discussion of roles and responsibilities appears later, it is really important to share some basic structural overviews to both clarify misconceptions and generate any questions that need to be addressed.

The information you share will be specific to your project, but there are some themes you will want to cover. First, simply explain the role of the SME in your project. It might be something like this:

Your role as a subject matter expert (SME) is vital to the success of our project. You will be our main resource when working on content-related issues, and without your input, our chances for getting this correct are limited at best. Curriculum development will be handled by the design team, and we want you to focus on the content and not worry about anything else.

It is also just as important to provide a brief overview of your role in the process:

My role in this project is to manage the course design process, and to take all of the content-related information you provide the group and turn it into courses. I am your main contact during this time, and it is my responsibility to see that this project is successful and that you feel like a full partner in this effort.

While these are just brief examples of how to get started, you may find that a much more detailed overview of each individual's role in the team is shared. This might include support staff and others in the design team who will be part of the project. You don't want individuals to appear out of nowhere and interact with your SMEs. No one should be a surprise to them at any part of this process. It breeds suspicion and erodes trust.

You don't want individuals to appear out of nowhere and interact with your SMEs.

Project Details

As soon as timelines, deadlines, deliverables, and other related information is available, it should be shared with your SMEs. At best, they will review the timelines and deadlines to get a feel for the timing of the project. Beyond that is probably wishful thinking in most cases, but you will have made the effort to be inclusive.

If you have a project management plan that includes key dates and deliverables, you may want to share all (or only relevant) elements with your group. Another document often requested by SMEs is an organizational chart that lists key personnel and their roles in the organization. In a consultant-led project, this would include both the client and the design firm's information. Often, your SME group has prior experience with someone in the organization that is not part of the design function, and these relationships can prove valuable down the line for both you and your content experts.

Background Materials

What you include as background material varies by each project. Some common items are grant proposals, existing courses and content information, outside consulting work and reports, accreditation reports, internal reports on training gaps, and thousands of other items.

It should be expected that your SME group may not spend much time with these materials, and don't be disappointed if later discussions don't include much of this from the SME side. Some of the materials may, however, prove useful once the project is underway, and you are working through the content with your experts.

You might also want to include some information on the ISD process and the ADDIE model for review. This would also be useful later if you decide to have an ISD boot camp (covered in a later chapter) for your SMEs. A short ISD primer like one of ASTD's *Infolines*, either "The Basics of ISD Revisited" or "Basics of Instructional Systems Development," might prove a great investment in sparking an interest in your SMEs.

Kickoff Meeting

No project is complete without a kickoff meeting of some sort. More importantly, no project starts off with a higher degree of potential success than when everyone has the same information and expectations. These meetings are not unique to projects with SMEs, but many times, fringe team members—in this case SMEs—are left out of these meetings, and the consequences to this oversight vary from poor communication to complete anarchy later in the project.

Some groups have formal and elaborate meetings that border on entertainment, while others have a less ceremonial approach by using a conference call or web meeting to get started. In either case, it is important that everything you need to get started is shared at this point and communicated with everyone involved in the project.

SMEs especially appreciate having the group take time to formally welcome them and bring them up to speed on the project, timelines, deadlines, and other particulars. This is also the perfect time to clear up any misconceptions, misinformation, and other possibly negative elements of the project.

Introductions, responsibilities, and other housekeeping issues need to take place at this point. It is also productive to introduce a set of ground rules the group will follow during the project.

Safety Valve

One useful aspect of welcoming your SMEs to the process is to make sure they have a way of letting someone know when there are problems that need to be addressed. Whether these are critical or just annoying to your content experts, there needs to be a safety valve that allows them to contact you or a prominent member of your team to resolve issues.

Table 4-2: Issues That May Trigger the Safety Valve

- Lack of responsiveness from training team to SME concerns.
- Late or nondelivery of promised materials.
- Consistent errors in materials provided to SMEs.
- Conflicting scheduling issues that remain unresolved.
- Personality conflicts with other SMEs or training team members.
- Professional differences with other SMEs that remain unresolved.
- Confusing or contradictory assignment specifics.
- Unrealistic travel expectations.
- Unrealistic participation expectations.
- Extension of time or participation commitment without consultation.
- Unequal balance of work among SMEs.
- Unprofessional treatment of SMEs by training team.
- Removal from SME role without consultation or advanced notice.
- Inability to continue participation due to personal issues not associated with work.
- Lack of promised technology or other support aids.
- Waning of interest or commitment to a project by SME.
- SME burnout.

Sometimes the mere knowledge that a safety valve exists is sufficient to have the desired effect of letting everyone know the door is always open. There is a quiet comfort in knowing a resource like this exists. It says a lot about your leadership and approach to managing the process when you acknowledge that problems might exist and that there is a mechanism to deal with them quickly before they fester and become larger than necessary.

Conclusion

You can never invest too much time in making your SMEs feel welcome and appreciated as they start working with you.

Discussion Questions

1. What are the advantages of taking the extra time to make SMEs feel welcome and appreciated before you actually start working on a project?

2. At the beginning of a project, which materials might be important for an SME to review before getting started? Is there anything you would not want to share with them?

3. Do you think it is important to have a kickoff meeting before starting any formal work on a project? What would you include in this meeting if you facilitated it?

 ## Case Study Question

You are beginning a small project that will include two or three SMEs working together several times to provide guidance on the content for a short four-hour course. What, if anything, would you do to get the project started with your SMEs?

Chapter 5

Defining Roles and Responsibilities

Chapter Objectives

At the end of chapter 5, you will be able to:

- Define and communicate SME roles and responsibilities.
- Define scope creep.
- List ways to address inaction within committees.

Chapter Overview

A training and instructional design project that starts without specific guidelines concerning roles and responsibilities within the group stands a good chance of facing confusion and misunderstanding among participants. This can easily be avoided by planning and communicating with your SMEs early and often about expectations within the project. This also serves to ease the minds of SMEs who think they are responsible for areas of the project that the design team will be addressing.

There is nothing worse than a training project that goes off the rails because no one is sure about their roles and responsibilities within the group. Without leadership and specific expectations, any project can quickly turn into organizational chaos. When working with SSMEs, this becomes even more pronounced, since time and resources are generally being shared. Any confusion or wasted effort is a negative that eventually feeds on itself.

Some of this depends on project management skills and time spent thinking through the process of how to get from point A to point B. However, for our purposes, it is important that the roles and responsibilities of our SMEs and design team are always at the forefront in our planning and execution. When working with SMEs, more unnecessary tension and anxiety comes from this aspect of the process than any other. No one likes to waste time. SMEs dislike it more than most, and this lack of planning can cost you not only time and credibility, it can also cost you lots of money if you are paying for or trading SME resources.

SME Roles

In chapter 1, we defined the various types of SMEs. Now we need to look at the specific roles each of these assets might play during a project. Each type of SME has a different set of expectations depending on their role, and while the same person may fill several different roles, their participation is different for each role. This is sometimes a point of confusion and frustration, often because the role expectations are not consistent with what is needed in a particular situation.

Each type of SME has a different set of expectations depending on their role, and while the same person may fill several different roles, their participation is different for each role.

As an example, an SSME may go into great detail about the content, while in a meeting that is designed to be an overview for a board or governing body. This level of detail is not necessary in this situation, and usually just creates tension between the design function and the SME. This is where a clear expectation of roles at the beginning of the project defuses this discussion. It allows the SSME to either participate more directly with the TSME group or work with the design team to address any issues before a meeting that is intended as an overview.

What you want to avoid at all costs is having SMEs assuming certain roles and working under assumptions that are in conflict with the expectations of the design team. The balance of too little and too much participation is always going to be a challenge, but in most cases this is a reasonable discussion, and solutions are available that are acceptable on both sides. What doesn't work is trying to change these roles after everyone is already engaged and thinking they are doing what is expected of them. The key is having these discussions before you start working with your SME groups, not after.

In most situations, expecting an SME to play any other role in a project without some prior experience or training opens the door to negative possibilities. It has the potential to be the training equivalent of an airline captain asking the passenger in 14C to fly the plane—not a chance most of us want to take. As in most group endeavors, a vacuum of leadership allows for unexpected outcomes. Since many SMEs are accomplished professionals before they join a project, it is instinctive for them to take on leadership roles, even if their experience and knowledge doesn't resonate with the reality of challenges in a training environment. Leadership doesn't always translate well from one professional scenario to another. Defining roles and responsibilities early allows people to discuss and resolve misunderstandings and turf issues before they kill momentum and place a project at risk.

In chapter 1, we defined the primary categories of SMEs as technical, hybrid, functional, instructional, and sentinel. Let's look at the way these different SME groups are likely to participate, and review ideas for how to best define and communicate their roles during a project.

Technical SMEs

TSMEs are the group that trainers and designers are most familiar with. These are the technical experts, and their primary role in the process is to see that the content portion of a deliverable is correct. They generally prefer to just be SMEs. But as we will see later, some may want to assume additional responsibilities during a project, and will even want to learn about and participate in more traditional training and design functions. For now, we will work with the idea that these SMEs will only participate as SMEs.

TSMEs should know and accept from the beginning that the non-content instructional design aspects of the project are the responsibility of others, and that their skills are needed in making sure the content is thoroughly illuminated and accurate. This clarity in role will lessen and usually eliminate many unrealistic expectations a

TSME might have about their role in the process. Being able to focus on the content provides a very directed environment for them to work within.

Some within this group of SMEs may be willing to shoulder additional roles in support of the design process. Ancillary roles include writing, taking photos, producing diagrams and other technical drawings, and doing research in areas that are not specifically covered by any of the SMEs. Not only does this allow for additional resources to be employed, it also has the potential to build the committee's engagement and enthusiasm for the project.

All too often, an issue arises where an SME feels they have enough experience in training or teaching to assist in the design process. There are occasionally individuals who are qualified to do this, but in most cases it is a point of friction within the group. Clearing up this role identification early—or at least having the discussion before it becomes a problem—is the best way to go. It may come down to everyone appreciating that content belongs to the SMEs, and instructional design belongs to the design team.

Table 5-1: TSME Role

SME Type	Key Attributes	Skills	Potential Issues and Solutions
TSME	• Focus on correcting content.	• Usually only like to participate as an SME. • Can pick up ancillary roles: writing, taking photos, producing diagrams and technical drawings, doing research in additional areas.	• Non-content ISD aspects should be the responsibility of others. • Sometimes, their prior experience in training or teaching makes them feel they should assist in the design process, which may be a point of friction.

Hybrid SMEs

When an SME is also going to implement a course (or already implements a course) there is a different level of expectations and ownership of the process. This is especially true if a course that exists is being reworked or migrated to a new method of implementation, like taking it online. This is also true when courses are being designed for another language, which always requires more than just translation.

In higher education, it is now a common practice to move classroom-based courses to an online environment, and the classroom instructor is expected to participate in the process of migrating the content to a learning management system (LMS). This move might involve building an online resource for course participants to use, or actually creating a course that is totally implemented online. In between these two extremes are various levels of blended courses, which involve a mix of online and in-class elements.

HSMEs have a different feeling of ownership over the process and product than a more traditional TSME. They feel entitled to a say in how a course is designed and ultimately how it will be implemented. They sometimes resent having to prepare new course designs, and they may participate in the process in a less-than-enthusiastic manner. Others will be excited to learn something new about course design and will participate actively. It just depends.

In either case, role expectations are equally as important in this environment as in any other scenario. Creating a working environment early in the process smoothes the way for collaboration throughout the project.

The scale of each project is something that varies by project. In academia it may range from one instructor moving a single course to an entire college, or a university deciding they want to offer online courses in numerous departments. In training environments, it is not unusual to see very large and successful legacy classroom-based programs being migrated online to reach organizational goals.

Table 5-2: HSME Role

SME Type	Key Attributes	Skills	Potential Issues and Solutions
HSME	• Entitled to a say in how the course is designed and in how it is ultimately implemented.	• Aids in any courses that need to be re-worked, translated, or migrated online. • Good at blended learning.	• Sometimes they resent having to prepare new course designs. • They also need role expectations clarified.

Instructional SMEs

One of the most important links in the implementation of a course is the facilitator. Sometimes they are called trainers, teachers, instructors, professors, or doctors. No matter the label, their subject matter expertise is often assumed, expected, or ignored.

Some would argue they are the most important component, since they can rescue a marginal course design and inspire and motivate learners exclusive of the content or delivery method. Within the ISD ranks, the ISME is the Rosetta stone that translates the course design into course implementation. To most learners, the ISME is the only contact they have with the course design process.

This group of SMEs is included here because they are often forgotten in the course design process other than some general reference to their existence, and in some cases, instructions to them on how to implement the course. It is imperative that designers work with this group to ensure a smooth transition from concept to course.

Often your TSMEs will also be ISMEs, but it is necessary to address each skill differently. Gathering content is different from making decisions about how to implement a course. There can also be differing opinions about how implementation should be accomplished within the TSME group that is beyond both their ability to determine and their influence to decide.

This is where being very clear about roles and responsibilities will allow a productive process. ISMEs are often incorporated as a source for information on what is likely to work best in a particular learning population. Questions concerning online versus classroom—and even basic questions related to module length and class size—are generally fair game, and limiting the discussions to these issues is a necessity. Having ISMEs revisit content and other aspects of the project kills time and has no boundaries. Keep it tight and focused with this group, and make sure everyone is onboard with the scope of their responsibility.

Table 5-3: ISME Role

SME Type	Key Attributes	Skills	Potential Issues and Solutions
ISME	• Translates the course design into course implementation. • To most learners, this is the only contact they have with the course design process. • Makes decisions about implementing a course.	• They can rescue a marginal course design and inspire and motivate learners exclusive of the content or delivery method.	• They are often forgotten, but they should be included to ensure a smooth transition from concept to course. • Don't have them revisit content and other aspects of the project. • Clarify scope of responsibilities.

Functional SMEs

Depending on the scope of your project, you may have an entire troop of FSMEs, or you may have none. In either case, you will certainly have tangible deliverables to be developed. This might be as simple as a series of handouts or slides if you are working alone. In more complex projects, you may have everything from graphic artists and programmers, to photographers and a film production crew.

Defining expectations and deadlines with these SMEs is as critical as any relationships you have during a project. They usually have, however, little or no knowledge of ISD or curriculum design and they think and communicate as experts in their domain.

One simple rule to remember in dealing with this population of experts is to get everything in writing and make sure that deliverables and deadlines are excruciatingly defined and documented. While certainly not an ISD or SME issue exclusively, they are SMEs and they do require the same level of relationship building as any other group of experts you deal with on a project.

SME Type	Key Attributes	Skills	Potential Issues and Solutions
Table 5-4: FSME Role			
FSME	• Could be graphic art-ist, program-mers, pho-tographers, or a film production crew.	• They think and communicate as experts in their domain.	• Define expectations and deadlines—very critical. • They usually have little or no knowledge of ISD. • Get everything in writing. • They require the same level of relation-ship building as any other experts.

Sentinel SMEs

Almost every project has some form of managerial or organizational oversight group. In some cases, this is simply one person charged with overall responsibility of a project. In many cases, there are boards that serve this purpose. For our purposes we are going to focus on the larger group function—a board.

The reason these SMEs are considered sentinels is because they generally have little to do with the actual design process. They are there to see that the work is complete to a (sometimes ambiguous) standard. These groups can be from many different organizations working on a combined project, or they can be part of a consortium that has received funding under a grant or other financial award.

SSMEs are seldom experts in the content, but are often high-ranking organizational representatives who have some managerial control over the functions related to the content. In the world of skills training, for example, an SSME might be the president of a company that employs workers with a specific skill. In the nonprofit world, a sentinel might be the executive director of the organization funding a project.

In most cases, the design function will be required to report and make sense of every aspect of the project, including content-related issues. When it comes to content, most of these sentinels do not have relevant subject matter expertise, yet they will ultimately make decisions relating directly to subject matter choices and treatment within the project. Many a designer has made presentations to this group, only to be helplessly whittled to nothingness over content issues that sentinels don't fully understand. In terms of role expectations with sentinels, it is necessary to confirm their role is not line-by-line edits on content and process, but instead is a more general overview that includes their advice and consent.

This is easier said than done with a group that is used to being heard. If there are personality or organizational histories and conflicts, these often show up in this venue. It takes a strong designer to mold this group into a supportive body when things go astray, for instance: A three-hour meeting is still deadlocked after seven hours.

Remember that SSMEs are experts at some level of content knowledge, but may not be detailed experts, or even current in their knowledge. Expectations need to be managed early in the process to keep this group functioning and supportive.

Table 5-5: SSME Role

SME Type	Key Attributes	Skills	Potential Issues and Solutions
SSME	• Managerial or organizational oversight group. • Generally have little to do with the actual design process. • Seldom experts in content.	• Will make decisions relating directly to subject matter choices.	• Arguments over content that sentinels don't fully understand. • Confirm that their role is not line-by-line edits on content and process. • Sometimes personality or organizational histories and conflicts occur with these SMEs.

Other Issues Related to Roles and Responsibilities

Later in the book as we look at evaluating SME performance, we will review factors that help us determine the best fit for each of our content experts. Before that discussion, it is important to visit some of the issues that may become problems within the relationship between SMEs and the design team.

Scope Creep With Content

When we talk about scope in this context, we talk about the defined area that a project or a specific area of content might involve. This is usually set by external factors like grant requirements, organizational priorities, or other fairly well-defined parameters.

You may encounter scope-creep issues related to how much content is really being included in a specific area of content. While a project plan might include review and revision of four modules of a specific course, the SME group might push for expansion of that coverage. They could argue that revising only four modules leaves the modules before and after the content out of date, or that these other modules need revision more than the chosen set.

In this situation the responsibility for the scope of the project has already been determined. Budget, resources, and organizations will have already made these decisions, and while the SME group might be correct in their judgment, the reality of the situation has already been decided. No amount of whining or pouting by anyone is going to change these decisions.

Having established and shared these guidelines early is part of the solution, but it also goes back to the acceptance of the roles each group plays in the process. The TSMEs will have little voice in this change, while the SSME group might address it, either directly or indirectly when it is raised as an issue. If the roles are clear, the course of action for adjudication is dictated by the structure of the project. Win, lose, or draw, the process must be honored.

Role Inflation

There are occasions when content experts take it upon themselves to assume a role not assigned to them within the team. There are times when this is helpful, such as taking pictures, writing some of the content, doing research, and reviewing large volumes of data that aren't in their original scope. This is generally well received and appreciated.

The other aspect of role inflation is when you see someone assume the office of CEO of the project. They attempt to dictate aspects of the process to others, including the project manager. Sometimes they are subtle and sometimes they are obvious. Each of these is handled differently based on the many factors involved, but to ignore this situation is to do so at your peril.

If you have set the roles and responsibilities early and communicated those to the SME group, you have plenty of options to work with. If you have avoided that conversation and have not made roles and responsibilities clear, you have a long road ahead to try to resolve this situation. But, you must address it and resolve it, or put your project at risk of becoming less productive.

If you have set the roles and responsibilities early and communicated those to the SME group, you have plenty of options to work with.

Inaction or Worse

Part of every new project and interaction with your SMEs should include a list of expectations and responsibilities. These only need to be basic elements of participation like meeting deadlines, taking on responsibilities, attending meetings, answering emails and calls, and all of the sundry items one can expect as an active content expert working on a project.

If everyone is clear about these expectations, the occasional ripple can be easily handled, and often a busy or uninterested SME can be quietly replaced without much tension or drama. Once in a great while, the more stubborn case of less-than-stellar performance will need to be addressed in a more assertive way, and your original list of expectations will serve as the starting point for those discussions.

There are also occasions where personal life issues affect the participation of a content expert, and they are not comfortable sharing what the issues are and how they might be resolved. I have seen some very sad and challenging situations be completely hidden because the atmosphere was not open enough to allow this conversation. Given the fact that many SMEs only work with us on one project—and then only occasionally during the process—this sheds light on the isolated nature of communication that can happen. Making this possibility part of your roles and responsibilities discussion at the beginning can provide some support if this happens.

◇◇

Conclusion

Defining roles and responsibilities when working with SMEs is sometimes the single most important element in starting a project correctly. Since many SMEs have never worked in this capacity before, they may have un-realistic—or even worse—no expectations about the roles they play in the process. There can also be a great deal of difference in an SME's role perception and the reality of the project as you work on it. Take the time to have this discussion and make sure that everyone agrees on the roles each person plays, and iron out any differences before getting started on the difficult work of the committee.

◇◇

Discussion Questions

1. What is the major responsibility of an SME in a curriculum design project?

2. Are there times when a design team has too high of expectations for SMEs?

3. Is there ever a time when an SME should be given traditional training and instructional design roles during a project?

 ## Case Study Question

You are halfway through a large design project, and you are having problems getting SMEs to meet deadlines and provide materials in the form expected for you to do your work. You haven't really been too specific about your expectations, since you are trying to create a healthy work environment to keep conflicts to a minimum. What do you think your next step should be to address the issues?

Chapter 6

Versions, Deliverables, and Deadlines

Chapter Objectives

At the end of chapter 6, you will be able to:

- Describe version control when working with SMEs.
- Describe deliverables needed when working with SMEs.
- Describe deadlines in working with SMEs.

Chapter Overview

Every project has challenges with keeping large volumes of documents and deliverables current and readily available to SMEs. Add to this the inevitable defining and meeting of deadlines, and you have many issues to consider as you work with SMEs.

SMEs are busy people—if in doubt, just ask them.

One thing they universally dislike (as do we all) is wasting time. This is exacerbated when an SME feels their time is being wasted by inefficiencies and a lack of attention to detail by the design team that could easily be avoided. The three most common areas of this frustration that I have seen relate in some way to document versions, deadlines, and deliverables.

In general, these three are the Achilles' heel of training projects. When working with SMEs, each of these can be the bane of your existence if you don't have a plan for how to manage them. It isn't enough to simply coordinate all of these activities; it takes a real pro to have these under control and to anticipate the problems content experts will experience if left to chance. Your SMEs are probably unfamiliar with the way you work, so you need to plan and communicate with them.

While this topic could easily constitute a whole book, our focus is on how this relates to our SMEs. We always want to make sure we are ahead of the roadblocks and have a plan that allows for the inevitable frustrations along the way. Remember that most content experts—especially first-time SMEs—are not familiar with how a training project works. The issues associated with these project management topics need this degree of attention in discussing how to build relationships with our content expert partners.

Version Control

Version control is the complex process of making sure everyone is working on the most recent version of a document or deliverable. Sometimes these are design documents, like skills inventories, objectives, or evaluation instruments. These can also be more tangible products like software, texts, visuals, storyboards, scripts, or any other aspect of the design process. With SMEs, these are most often drafts of chapters or modules and may contain diagrams, drawings, photos, or other specific content.

On large projects which often have more than one person contributing and commenting on a single draft, make sure you have a system in place for working on the same draft version—it becomes critical. As you would expect, the more complex your project environment, the more people have their hands in the mix. Every hand creates another opportunity for mistakes in versions. You must make sure that each SME is working with the most recent version of every document.

Imagine that you are an SME and have been asked to review documents that contain specific information related to a complex safety device. This device is going to be part of a new training program for power plant operators. After receiving the materials and taking several hours to review and write up comments on the best way to train operators on the device, you attend a meeting to discuss the process and everyone else seems to be working from a more recent draft. Anyone in this situation would ask "Why bother?" One rendering or another of this story happens to SMEs way too often during training projects, but it is avoidable.

The reason version control is so important is because the further away content experts are from day-to-day activity in the design process, the more likely they are to be momentarily forgotten in the document-handling side of the equation. "Out of sight, out of mind" is more than just a saying in busy offices and during complex projects. You have to make version control a priority and ensure everyone is both aware of and following the required guidelines.

You have to make version control a priority and ensure everyone is both aware of and following the required guidelines.

Version Control Options

Before you decide on a system for version control, you need to commit to having one person responsible for managing the process. This guardian of the process will ultimately be the one who works with your SMEs to ensure compliance with procedures, and follows up with your group to make sure everyone is on the same page—literally.

Once you agree to a guardian, you now need to decide which procedure works best for your situation. This will depend on what types of documents you are working on and where your content experts are located. The ideal situation is everyone working in the same office or in close proximity, but that is the exception and not the rule, from my experience.

Dispersed groups are best served by an online file storage system that allows everyone access. There are numerous commercial options, and you can also maintain documents on private servers if your organization has this capacity. Make sure everyone has login instructions, including the required username and password. As you get started, rest assured a healthy percentage of your group will lose, forget, or not understand how to use any of the information, so your guardian will need to troubleshoot or contact the help desk as required.

Numbering systems are key to making any version-control system work. There are date systems, initial systems, date and initial systems, and systems that combine a sequential version number into the scheme.

Date systems can be as easy as file names that include the date and time: 02_14_2015_9_38am.

To people, this means February 14, 2015 at 9:38 am was the last time the file was saved. For this system to work, each file must be closed with a file name that has been updated with the correct information. Miss this once, and the system starts to fail until corrected.

It is also acceptable to use a personal initials system with date and time: ckh_2_14_2015.

This approach allows for more personalization and helps identify who opened and closed the file. For either of these approaches, you can add or subtract information to make the file names meet your needs. You also should make sure files can be saved with file names this length, and containing the characters you want to use.

A third approach is designating versions by numbers alone: Ver1.0 followed by Ver1.1—and so on.

For this system to work, everyone has to pay attention to what they start with and what they end with in terms of the version number. You can add dates and initials to make this more specific.

It is also possible to make all available files PDFs that can't be modified, to ensure master files are not changed. While it is true that most systems record the date and time of the most recent saving of a file, this isn't a reliable way to ensure correct versions, since there are many issues with multiple people accessing the same file at different times. For example, someone can download a file and not check back with the system for updates, and then be several versions behind before they put their edited file back in the management system.

Deliverables

The tangible and process-related artifacts of a project are usually defined as deliverables. Each project has a unique angle on this, but you should always define the term and what constitutes a deliverable early in the process. Without deliverables you have no need for deadlines, and while this seems ridiculously simple—or unnecessary— there is a large risk of misunderstanding expectations in the absence of this element.

Deliverables, from my experience, fall into the general categories of tangible and process-related. Tangible deliverables are draft and final versions of objectives, skill-task analysis, evaluations, content, photos, diagrams, reference materials, software products like project media, storyboards, lesson plans, learning management system course sections, and anything else that has a physical presence. If you can see it or touch it, you have a tangible deliverable.

Process-related deliverables are meeting dates and times, conference call schedules, phone calls, emails, web-based meetings, or anything that lacks a physical presence but still has a deadline or schedule attached to it. While you might argue that process-related elements don't qualify as deliverables, you need to consider that most frustration in this process has its genesis in a project that does not have all of the elements of communication firmly managed and planned. All of these require commitment and agreement to be useful, and they are deliverables in every sense of the term.

All process-related elements such as meetings and conference calls require commitment and agreement to be useful, and they are deliverables in every sense of the term.

Deadlines

One of the key elements of project management and working with SMEs is establishing and maintaining deadlines. These can be for deliverables, reading and review assignments, writing, photos, gathering materials, and just about any other part of the project. Every project participant will have different thoughts on deadlines, and you can only ignore addressing these at your own peril.

When you work with busy content experts who are likely to have a whole other world of work and deadlines to satisfy in addition to your priorities, deadlines have an additional level of detail. Finding the right balance is a moving target that will change from group to group, and even from deliverable to deliverable within each project.

There are often two competing strategies in dealing with deadlines for SMEs: too tight or too loose. Too tight a deadline, and you have upset team members and many missed deadlines. Too loose, and you watch as weeks go by when nothing appears to be happening, since nothing is due or expected.

Great projects will have a third strategy that expects the process of deadline selection to be a dynamic rather than static process. Each deadline is different based on the variables and individuals involved. This seems obvious, but the reality of making this work is more complicated than appears at a distance, and working with your SMEs on deadlines is always better than assigning them without discussion.

Today Is the...

How many deadline discussions have started with someone saying something related to the present date? It's as if to say "two weeks from today" or "by the end of next week" is the best time for a deadline. One thing we know for sure is that deadlines need to be realistic, and based on an average of the time each SME thinks is reasonable to complete a specific deliverable.

To-Do Lists for SMEs

The dreaded to-do list is often the thread that keeps the timing of a project on pace. Having each deliverable with an accompanying person of responsibility and set date and time for delivery is absolutely necessary. There are as many versions of this as there are SMEs and trainers, but the focus is the same; keeping everything on target and having a person of responsibility assigned to each task.

Project management techniques aside, here are some basics to consider. The following example is only one way to do this.

Table 6-1: Task List for SMEs

Task	Due Date	Primary Responsibility	Secondary Responsibility	Completed Date

Here is an example with data entered into each column for a project with multiple modules, involving a skill-based task for content. ISD stands for the instructional designer, SME is the content expert committee, and individual names followed by SME are individual content experts.

Table 6-2: Task List Example for SMEs

Task	Due Date	Primary Responsibility	Secondary Responsibility	Completed Date
Prepare draft task sequencing for module 100a	7-15	ISD	SME committee A	7-10
Write objectives for module 100a	7-21	ISD		7-21
SME meeting to review module 100a	7-22	ISD	SME committee A	7-22
Research content for module 101a	7-29	M. Schmidt - SME	ISD	
Prepare draft task sequencing for module 101a	8-15	ISD	SME committee B	
Write objectives for module 101a	8-22	ISD		

Conclusion

Taking the time to attend to project details goes a long way in building a positive and lasting relationship with your SMEs.

Discussion Questions

1. What is the best way to handle the numerous versions of documents that each project contains?

2. Do you keep an active list of deliverables when you are working on a design project? Why or why not?

3. How much success do you have making and keeping deadlines? What are the problems that you have faced and how did you resolve them?

Case Study Question

It is your first design project and you realize the scale of the project is going to demand that you pay a lot of attention to how you will arrange and manage the process of sharing documents and materials. How will you plan the process, and what are your major concerns as you get started?

Chapter 7

Evaluating SME Performance

Chapter Objectives

At the end of chapter 7, you will be able to:

- Describe a system for rating SME contributions.
- Design a rubric for operationalizing the evaluation of SMEs.

Chapter Overview

Evaluating each of your SMEs is a necessary part of managing a project, and having tangible guidelines for this process makes the job a little easier.

Once you have your TSMEs selected and working in your project, it is now the time to start a systematic evaluation of their contributions. There are several ways to do this, and you can find the best fit for your situation.

If you want to have very detailed data for reviewing your content experts, you can use a matrix of criteria relevant to your project, and rate each SME accordingly. The specific criteria you use can vary from this model, but the focus of the process is the same either way.

Content Knowledge

Begin by listing the expectations within your project that relate to your SME's content knowledge. In a typical project, these might include

- relevance of content knowledge
- depth of content knowledge
- accuracy of content knowledge
- timeliness of content knowledge.

We have already talked a lot about these, but let's add details as they relate to the review and rating process.

Relevance of Knowledge

Nothing is worse than having your first meeting with your SME or group of SMEs and discovering that despite your preparation and attention to résumés and other data, one of your content experts is clearly in over his head. The symptoms of this are generally pretty obvious; they either avoid commenting, or they agree with others without providing any original input. With these criteria, an SME can miss by a mile and it will eventually be obvious to everyone.

In thinking about these criteria you need to be liberal in your early judgments, since there may be more than just content knowledge at work. I have seen many talented content experts become overwhelmed by the environment they experience the first time as part of the curriculum design process. They are not sure how to communicate or what they are really supposed to contribute in meetings. While your pre-meeting preparation (with a kickoff and background materials) will help, there are occasions where our SME just needs to settle in to this process, which may be completely foreign to her professional experience.

Depth of Knowledge

If you have an SME who doesn't go beyond occasional generic comments, and makes contributions that appear very pedestrian and not topic specific, then this SME usually lacks deep knowledge. Look for a lack of connectivity between simple and complex levels of detail, and for posturing comments that reflect a need to "read up on that" before offering any input. One example of an SME with a depth-of-knowledge challenge is a person who clearly has a basic understanding of local building codes for the installation of electrical systems, but seems lost when asked about codes relating to a specific type of wind turbine installation—which is the content you are preparing.

If you feel that you have as much or more insight into the content conversation as an SME, then your instincts say that you have someone who is not going to contribute much to at least this aspect of the discussion. This of course can change from one specific content point to another depending on the complexity of the discussion. This may be situational in some or all of your SMEs, depending on how much material you expect to cover with one group of experts. You are looking for a pattern of limited engagement and complexity with the content across the breadth of your project.

Remember that even content experts have varied knowledge on specific topics, and when surrounded by others who may have more experience, they are likely not to contribute much of value. This can change with the next topic, and the tables can turn completely on which SME is leading and contributing.

With the depth and relevance criteria, it is often better to allow a break-in period before becoming concerned about an individual SME. Environmental factors may influence them early in the process, and these factors may mitigate after brief adjustments within the group and each expert.

Timeliness of Knowledge

This criterion is sometimes the easiest to determine and sadly, it is often the most personable and interesting content expert in your group who fails in this area. A person's longevity or faithful service, and the power of some personalities, causes them to be selected to serve as an SME in many situations.

For example, Steven has been part of the organization for 35 years, and everyone likes him without reservation. It is considered an honor to serve on this committee for the important new project, and this is Steven's chance to savor some of the attention he probably really deserves. However—and I hate to say this—perhaps our honored colleague is not the best choice.

In these situations, you sometimes must ignore the obvious and use the goodwill that flows from having Steven on the committee or working on the project. There are worse things that can happen, and you can take this valuable organizational asset and turn it into a plus with a little imagination and acceptance of reality.

There is also the chance that an SME may have been serving in an administrative role, or some other staff function that didn't require staying current with the content.

The general feeling that vocational longevity equates to universal operational knowledge seldom proves true. These are difficult decisions to make, and often we just have to live with them to keep peace and not appear to be unappreciative.

As you chart these criteria, you can start with this framework. It is similar to the selection criteria tables, but with some different categories. Perhaps your rating changed as you worked with them.

Table 7-1: Evaluating SMEs

Name	Relevance	Depth	Accuracy	Timeliness	Total
WEF	1	1	2	3	7
MRT	2	3	3	2	11

Scale is 0 to 3 with 0 designating no knowledge, 1 designating a minimum knowledge, 2 designating an average knowledge, and 3 designating superior knowledge. NA designates no relevance for this project.

Preparedness

One facet of SME participation that affects every part of the design process is the ability and willingness of a content expert to be prepared for meetings, deliverables, and other mandated points of production in a project. There are multiple key areas that should be on everyone's list, and you will probably add several that are specific to your needs.

Some basic preparedness criteria include

- reads and reviews requested materials
- comments as required
- supplies materials as required
- meets deadlines
- returns emails and calls
- attends meetings.

Let's look at each individually and see how they fit into our review.

Reads and Reviews

It is almost impossible to meet any deadlines or get any traction in a project if you have any member of the team not keeping up with the read-and-review process. There are projects where this is the prime expectation of the SMEs, and it is vital everyone keeps up. This is sometimes a challenge for busy professionals, but there needs to be a balance between deadlines and expectations.

If you lack follow-through, your project and the other SMEs will be on hold until everyone catches up, and that creates an entire set of consequences that can ripple through your team. As you review this criteria, be honest with yourself about whether reasonable deadlines and expectations were initially made, and if the lack of follow-through is based at least partially on unrealistic expectations.

Comments as Required

Linked almost permanently to the criterion of read and review is the requirement that some tangible action take place after the read-and-review process is completed. It is incredibly easy for someone to say they have kept up with their read-and-review assignments if they aren't required to provide any tangible work as a result.

To make sure work was completed, request an edited document or a sign off of the materials, edits, and changes. While it is entirely possible to mark your initials on a document that you haven't actually reviewed as required, the results will always at some point appear as an obvious lack of effort. Later, when discussing why the team decided to do something a certain way, someone may be out of the loop because they did not actually complete the review. While eventually embarrassing for them, it does make for good theater if you have done your paperwork and can display the review and approval documentation.

Supplies Materials

Almost every SME committee meeting and process requires submitting deliverables to the project, whether a document, photo, diagram, chart, or one of a thousand other types of project artifacts. As these deliverables are assigned and accepted by the SME, you must establish a due date. You are measuring whether they honor the due date with the requested deliverable.

There are several ways that this becomes a problem. The first is when due dates are either ignored or are constantly moved back. This indicates that either there is a problem with the scheduling or there is a problem with follow-through on the part of the SME. It shouldn't be difficult to identify patterns here.

Also, sometimes you will receive deliverables that are deficient in expected quantity or quality, and will be detrimental to the project. While somewhat subjective, if you have clearly defined deliverables and deadlines, this is rather basic in interpretation.

Meets Deadlines

While somewhat connected to the supplies criterion, this is a more broad-based review of the ability of an SME to meet—and hopefully beat—any project deadlines. Sometimes these are deliverables that have fixed and defined expectations, and at other times, deadlines are related to process issues such as making team decisions or holding a conference call or webinar.

A pattern of not meeting deadlines and not being particularly concerned about missing them sends a very strong message about mission and attitude. Once one team member starts this pattern, others realize they can do the same, and everyone starts to lose traction and focus.

Returns Emails, Calls, and Other Communication

This is so self-explanatory that it really doesn't need much detail, but the importance can't be understated. The SME who plays hard to get and hard to find will eventually cause you a problem. This behavior might be a symptom of passive aggressive behavior aimed at no one in particular, but intended to send the message that he isn't at your immediate beck and call. It can also be as simple as a very busy person not able to keep up with demands on his time.

You should investigate to make sure you have the correct contact information, and that it is the preferred contact information. Many times, SMEs have multiple emails and phone numbers, and the SME can't even keep up with their information. I have seen this when I ask someone for their phone number and they have to think about it. Your communication issues might be just an innocent error in information. It's always best to check.

Attends Meetings

The most obvious vote against your project by an SME is his failure to attend your meetings. These can take place in person down the hall, by webinar or conference call, or can require travel from one end of the country to another. SMEs vote with their presence and this one is pretty obvious.

If your SME is too busy to attend, she really isn't doing you much good. If all you need is sign-off, then perhaps you can make this work. In any case, you need to determine the impact of her lack of attendance and note this in your review.

If you find other criteria that are important to you and that you want to include in this review, be sure to add them.

Here is what we talked about in chart form:

Table 7-2: Example SME Evaluations

Name	Reads Reviews	Comments	Supplies	Deadlines	Returns Emails/Calls	Attends Meetings	Total
WEF	3	3	0	2	3	3	14
MRT	3	3	3	2	2	2	15

Scale is 0 to 3 with 0 designating no preparedness, 1 designating a minimum preparedness, 2 designating an average preparedness, and 3 designating superior preparedness. NA designates no relevance for this project.

Intangibles

There are always criteria that relate more to attitude than anything as objective as knowledge or preparedness. This might be considered the "plays well with others" point of comparison, but it is important and sometimes critically so, depending on the tenor of the group and project.

Several criteria serve as a starting point for this area:

- leadership
- team player
- cooperative
- supportive
- volunteers
- focused.

While a review of the criteria might seem obvious—although a bit subjective—let's look at each and determine if they fit your needs for review and rating.

Leadership

This is one of my all-time favorite discussions with students and colleagues, and it usually centers around how you define leadership. Thousands of books and articles have been written about this, and every day somewhere there is a seminar on developing your own leadership or finding and nurturing this quality in others. There are designations such as formal leaders and informal leaders, and the classifications and definitions go on and on. In the end, you only need to determine if an SME is capable of providing leadership in some form for your project. This shouldn't become so complicated that you have to hire an SME to determine whether you have a leader in your group of SMEs.

Usually, this evolves with reasoned and informed comments during discussions, and the ability to find consensus in the SME group where differences appear. Leaders in this environment nudge rather than push their ideas, and they listen and comment without appearing patronizing.

Leaders take responsibility for deliverables and actually deliver them on time. They facilitate discussions that lead to making decisions, and they build a sense of purpose and commitment, often without saying anything specific. You know you have a leader when the group starts acting productively and professionally.

Team Player

You will always know an SME team player by their demeanor and participation within the group. They will leave their ego outside the door and often take one for the team by accepting responsibility for the more mundane and perfunctory tasks.

This is more than just volunteering or being supportive, which we will look at next. This is tied to wanting to be a part of something bigger than themselves, and looking at the predominately intrinsic rewards of being involved in the project. A team player is not looking for recognition or reward, rather simply participating to better the process or product.

Cooperative

Cooperation is important on any team. This differs from other elements of this review because it represents a universally held feeling by the SMEs that they will do what is asked. This is true of a leader, team player, or any other person in the group.

Cooperation is also displayed as the ability to facilitate assignments and discussions within the group if a roadblock develops. You will also see the cooperative SME helping out with small, sometimes non-content process issues like arranging tables or helping carry boxes.

Supportive

When thinking about this criterion, I often review the attitude that an SME carries into the work, especially when they work with the group in person or online in a synchronous meeting. This is the quality of being a cheerleader for the process. If you hear someone talking about the outcomes of the process and the bigger picture issues, then you have a supportive SME.

Volunteers

Like all of the other criteria, volunteering is a subjective judgment on your part, but in some ways more subjective, since it is the relative value of the volunteering that becomes important. For example, an SME may volunteer for many aspects of the project that don't really relate to the content. This could signal an issue that the content-related issues are less important than the others. In other words, someone volunteers to keep the focus off of his content contributions.

On the other side of this element is the fact that someone may honestly feel like taking on the extra burdens to get the project completed in a way that makes everyone satisfied. Again, very subjective, but worth a moment of reflection on what is really taking place within an individual SME.

Focused

I think we all know lack of focus when we see it. It may present itself as little if any participation, or a constant checking of the watch or laptop. This happens to everyone at some point or another, but it is the overriding lack of focus that should concern you and may warrant a lower rating on your rubric.

Table 7-3: Intangibles

Name	Leadership	Team Player	Cooperative	Supportive	Volunteers	Focused	Total
WEF	2	1	2	2	1	2	10
MRT	1	2	3	2	1	3	12

Scale is 0 to 3 with 0 designating no display of the criterion, 1 designating a minimum display of the criterion, 2 designating an average display of the criterion, and 3 designating superior display of the criterion. NA designates no relevance for this project.

Negatives

As an option, you may want to look at a final block of criteria, and these relate directly to negatives that may appear in one or more of your SME group. All of these should only be used as a basis for determining if a specific issue warrants intervention, or if it can just be considered a nuisance. This is not to insinuate that content experts display any of these tendencies more than any other professionals—or the design team itself—but you may need to chart every aspect of your relationship with SMEs to manage the process.

As you review these traits, you should determine if charting these works for you and if so, what you will add or subtract from the list. Our review will only discuss how these specifically relate to our training environment. Our criteria in this category are:

- patronizing
- demanding
- must lead
- rude
- late
- tech-bound.

Patronizing

When someone talks down to people or represents themselves as a step above the rest in terms of their knowledge or experience, they are being patronizing toward others in the group. Any team member who has a patronizing attitude toward one or more of the group has potential to be a problem. You will often see this with comments like "You should know that," or "We always do it that way—don't you?"

Within TSME groups, this behavior has potential downsides that directly affect participant quality, and therefore the information quality you receive from the group. First, if a content expert discounts other opinions, you will soon find that participation slows to a crawl, if it proceeds at all. Most others in this environment don't want to fight through the attitude of someone like this to express an opinion.

Also, sometimes there are heated discussions and short tempers over issues of relative unimportance. The point becomes winning an argument, not contributing a professional opinion about the content.

If someone has a well-known reputation for this kind of behavior, it might be less of a problem, since most people will just ignore it. However, a new or unknown SME with this attitude can kill a project's momentum very quickly.

Demanding

There is a thin line between demanding behavior and leadership. Sometimes demanding behavior will come across as an expectation that someone or everyone will do what an individual wants, as opposed to a leadership approach of having high expectations for performance from everyone. You will often see this across the board with an individual and not just in one scenario. For example, someone will not like the meeting room and then not like the coffee and the noisy environment.

Within the TSME committee, demanding behavior quickly reduces the efforts of support staff and instructional designers. Their jobs become about fighting each new fire that rises when everything isn't perceived to be perfect, instead of handling the rest of their work. Tension will eventually rise, and it isn't uncommon for even reasonable requests to be ignored or the response time considerably slowed. In either case, little gets done on the work at hand for the committee.

While not the worst quality to have to endure in a team member, it certainly can have an increasing impact over time and will eventually cause problems if left unaddressed.

Must Lead

To be honest, an SME who is used to being in charge is perhaps going to expect to be in charge, even while serving on a committee or working on a team that he does not manage. This tension will exist when decisions need to be made, and may surface when other negative issues exist in the group that are perceived to be ignored.

The person who must lead is often a frustrated individual who hasn't been asked to be in charge, but has been asked to be a team member—perhaps seen as a demotion in her eyes. Another way to tell if this behavior is leadership or must lead is to observe whether compromise is sought by this individual. A leader will seek and support compromise, while the must-lead individual will be unhappy if her position is not upheld.

In your committee, this TSME will often act to undermine the leadership of the committee and the project. He is sure he can do it better, and anything less than complete capitulation to his suggestions renders your leadership as lacking, and he won't be afraid to go over your head and make any waves he can to prove he is still connected and relevant. This can be a committee killer, and usually has to be dealt with in a permanent way unless the individual can be convinced to cease the bad behavior.

Rude

We all know rudeness when we see it. This quality is hardly restricted to content experts or any group for that matter. It is a team killer and a momentum stopper.

There are times when rude behavior is spawned by insecurity, and this acting out is an effort by an individual to bluff through a content or process they are not qualified to discuss. You might want to see if that is a possibility, since this is much more easily managed than dealing head on with an individual who is just rude by nature.

Rudeness is sometimes just what it is and not meant to be something personal or worse. Some folks are just rude by nature or environment. This can usually be ignored or addressed with humor.

Late

Being late is more than just arriving after everyone else. The habitually late individual becomes a symptom of a lack of leadership if it is allowed to continue. Charting this behavior will allow you different options if action is necessary.

**Charting this behavior will allow you different
options if action is necessary.**

Some individuals are just late all of the time. Others are acting out in a passive-aggressive manner to voice their opinions or concerns about an endless list of possible problems within the group or project.

In your committee, this behavior is nothing short of a disaster if it is consistent and of a long duration. Five minutes late one time is not the same as an hour late every time. This is something that has to be dealt with quickly and decisively.

Tech-Bound

The first cell phone ushered in the era of tech-bound professionals, including busy SMEs. With texting and various social media now residing on every smartphone, laptop, and tablet, you have the potential to have SMEs constantly paying more attention to technology than to anything or anybody else, including your project. If you have SMEs who are also consulting on other projects, this can rise to the level of ridiculous.

This is a real problem in instructional design environments, and just about everyone knows where the limits reside except the tech-bound person. From the embarrassing ringtones and Bluetooth earpiece to the constant text alerts, these SMEs can push any meeting into chaos. It can be regulated, and documenting the issues helps down the line in dealing with the issue should it become a problem.

If the problem is consistent and unrelenting, it needs to be documented. This is also a great item for your kickoff meeting and the list of ground rules for the SME committee. If you don't care, fine. If you do, make sure everyone knows the expectations related to phones, tablets, laptops, and other devices.

Case Study: Establishing a Self-Evaluation Atmosphere With SMEs

A large training organization was having problems finding a way to evaluate the many SMEs that they had working on different projects. Without a standard way to review SME participation, most of the evaluations were negative, since no mechanism for reviews had been established and the only comments they were hearing were negative. With the focus on negative performance reviews, SMEs were quickly opting out of future participation and even leaving current roles within a project. Something had to change, since there were very few real issues with the SME group, but all that they were hearing were less than positive comments on timeliness and quality of contributions from the design team.

To solve the lack of any real evaluation process, the organization adopted a 360-degree review framework that included not only the SMEs but also the entire training team. In this way, all participants and processes were open to review and comment. No topic or element of the project was considered off limits for these discussions.

The first step was to open the review and comment process to the SMEs, where they were free to share any thoughts they had on the process and decisions that affected their participation. This was done both in meetings and by email and online surveys. Since the initial focus was not on the SMEs themselves, this allowed the process to begin without SMEs feeling like they were under undue scrutiny. As these discussions were held, the training team would comment on any general concerns they had about SME participation without naming or pointing toward any individual SME. Any necessary follow-up with a specific SME was done confidentially offline. As it ended up, this was rarely—if ever—needed.

Shifting the focus away from the SMEs and opening the door to discussions on any aspect of the project cleared the air and allowed for real trust in the project team and the SMEs. The design team also learned a lot about how to work most effectively with SMEs when specific points of conflict were discussed and resolved. These problems generally pertained to all SMEs and the project teams quickly avoided the problem areas in future work with SMEs.

None of these behavioral traits are unique to any group, and your documentation of these issues is not an attempt at playing amateur therapist or providing the latest offering of reality TV psychobabble. However, you must protect the environment that you manage in this process, and if your SME group—or any team member—needs a reminder that some of these behaviors are not assisting the group, then you have the documentation to make your case in a professional and impersonal way.

Table 7-4: Negative Qualities

Name	Patronizing	Demanding	Must Lead	Rude	Late	Tech-bound	Total
WEF							
MRT							

As we have discussed the various aspects of SME evaluation, we have segmented each general area of criteria and provided tables within each segment. Now let's assemble one evaluation form that covers all of the areas we want to evaluate.

Table 7-5: Evaluating SMEs

Name:				Date:
Rating	**0**	**1**	**2**	**3**
CRITERIA				
Content:				
Relevance				
Depth				
Accuracy				
Timeliness				
Preparedness:				
Reads/Reviews				
Comments				
Supplies				
Deadlines				
Returns Coms				
Att. Mtgs				
Intangibles:				
Leadership				

Team Player				
Cooperative				
Supportive				
Volunteers				
Focused				
Negatives:				
Patronizing				
Demanding				
Must Lead				
Rude				
Late				
Tech-Bound				
Total				

Conclusion

Having criteria to review the participation of SMEs is a valuable asset in the process of designing curriculum. This is true both for the very objective review of content-based criteria and the more subjective review of non-content criteria. The degree to which you review your SMEs, or if you decided instead not to review their performance, will depend on your individual situation. In either case, having some background on what is expected and required in this arena will make you a better trainer and instructional designer.

Discussion Questions

1. In your review of your SMEs, you find a pattern of average content-based criteria rating that is much lower than you anticipated. What do think might be taking place?

2. You are finding that your SMEs are spending a lot of time on non-content discussions, and appear to be treading water instead of making progress on defining the content. What should you look for in your reviews to draw some conclusions about what is going on?

3. Your most-liked SME is adding almost nothing to the substantive content-related discussions within your committee. Is there any place in your review that helps find the source of the problem?

Case Study Question

You are leading a project in a very technical content area, and your SME committee will be spending a year working together on this project. They meet every several weeks in person and then correspond by email the rest of the time. After about three months you are seeing a real drop-off in participation by several key members of the group. You have decided not to ask for a chairperson or other SME leadership, and the burden is falling on you for all of the communication and work outside the in-person meetings. What are your options to pull this back together, and what are the possible causes of the issues?

Chapter 8

Problem Solving in SME Committees

Chapter Objectives

At the end of chapter 8, you will be able to:

- Identify typical problems in SME committees.
- Determine options for gaining access to SMEs.
- Suggest solutions for scheduling conflicts.
- Negotiate SME availability as necessary.
- Determine options for solving lack of participation issues in an SME.
- Evaluate and offer solutions for technology inequities within SMEs.
- Provide options for addressing deadlocked SME committees.
- Determine the best way to address personality conflicts within your SMEs.

Chapter Overview

Working with SME committees can be a challenge if you are not used to the environment. In this chapter we look at several common issues that arise in these situations.

In the process of working with SMEs, there are many issues that need to be addressed by the design team. Most of these are not necessarily unique to SMEs, but the ways to deal with them are often different in this environment, and thinking about them from a different angle might help in finding workable solutions.

Typical Problems

In my years of working in this environment, I have noticed a range of issues that are common in working cooperatively with SMEs. There isn't one solution for each issue, but there is often a familiar theme associated with each issue that allows for some common approaches to problem solving. This is not a complete list, since that is nearly impossible, but we will look at the most common from my experience.

Access to SMEs

The most universally experienced challenge that exists with SMEs is our ability to secure the services of our content experts when and where we need them. The variables in this situation are endless, but problems usually center around the specifics of who, when, and for how long.

If an SME is a freelance consultant, this is usually a matter of negotiating these variables to everyone's satisfaction. As with any contractual arrangement, these are subject to budget, availability, and other issues specific to the SME and to your requirements. The more difficult access issues are almost always related to internal or loan SMEs.

Internal and loan SMEs are those professionals who either work for your organization or are employed by an organization that is working with you on a project. This can be further complicated in the apprenticeship arena, since SMEs may work within a specific trade—such as an electrician or brick layer—but may be employed by multiple employers, depending on where their skills are needed at any specific time. They may also be employed by a joint training program as an apprenticeship instructor, and have rigorous teaching responsibilities that leave little time for any outside work.

If an SME is on loan from one department or organization to a project, the issue of in-kind participation and other issues may arise. These are generally best handled by the HR function, but the practical side of this issue for you is to ask how long you can expect to have the services of the SME, and whether you have any flexibility in when they are available. Tensions can arise when competing priorities exist between the SME's permanent responsibilities and the demands of the project.

Then you have the issues directly related to who is paying for expenses, lost time, and other costs not specifically related to any training function or project.

Scheduling Conflicts

Arranging meetings, conference calls, web meetings, and even phone calls can be a full-time job in some projects. Busy people are very difficult to schedule. If you are only dealing with one person, imagine trying to schedule something across time zones, thousands of miles, and even other continents.

The obvious first step is to try and find some compromise on the best times and days that work for the majority of your committee members. This has to take into account the fact that there may be shift-work issues, travel, vacation, religious obligations, time zones, and other complications to consider. Asking SMEs to meet on their own time at night or scheduled time and days off is always a problem. This can also be affected by any collective bargaining agreements that address overtime and other working conditions that might be related to meetings.

Asking SMEs to meet on their own time at night or scheduled time and days off is always a problem.

At best, you will arrive at some compromise, and in some cases you will need to have more than one meeting to cover the same project issues just to make sure you get full participation. This is a necessity in some cases and should just be considered one of the variables to be addressed.

You will probably find that the more you plan ahead by trying to incorporate everyone's needs, the more your schedules will become workable for the group. It is common for groups to struggle in the beginning to get everyone on a conference call or web meeting, but after several weeks, everyone starts to plan ahead and move other obligations out of the way to participate in your meetings.

There are those who argue that changing the day and time often works best for their groups. Others will argue the exact opposite and have a very rigid schedule. Neither is right or wrong, but you have to find what works best for your group and still keep your sanity within the committee. You also need to be open to the possibility that one or more of your SMEs may not be able to make schedules based on your preferred choices, and will need to be replaced or have marginal participation.

SME Availability

The ebb and flow of availability of SMEs is a problem faced by every design team at one point or another. Sometimes this manifests in missing scheduled meetings and other group sessions, and at other times it is missed deadlines and assignments.

The common point of frustration in most of these situations is that you are dealing with a person who doesn't report to you directly. You often feel that everything you do with your SMEs has to be finessed, and that very little in terms of reliable time available for them to work with you is set in stone.

While we would all like to think that we can negotiate the terms of the use of our SMEs and negate most of these issues—and there are times when you can—more often than not this landscape is constantly changing and it takes patience and compromise to make this work reliably. You can't let this become something that is held against the SME, or even their decision makers, since we are borrowing a valuable resource that is missed when not available.

Lack of Participation

On occasion you will find that one or more SMEs will simply not engage in the process of working on the content with the committee. The causes for this vary, from not wanting to work on the project, to being over their head with the content. You might also find that introversion, social skills, and other personality issues are at play.

Since SME resources are so scarce and usually expensive, you may have to make some tough decisions about continuing to work with someone who essentially does nothing more than show up. There are the occasional SMEs who have little to say until a critical moment in your work when they kick in and save the day for the group. They might have been bored and found nothing to contribute until they were challenged, or had the best information or ideas to share.

This is a very subjective problem to diagnose, and it takes time to figure out for sure what is taking place. Over time this will become obvious and you may have to make some changes to get the right person in position.

Technological Inequities

Increasingly, it is more visible in some projects that inequity of specific technologies is considered as important for working with your SMEs during a project. For example, some projects rely heavily on web-based conferencing, which requires—at a minimum—reliable Internet access and specific software or app. A headset or other equipment might also be required for full participation, plus the ability to view files during the conference. While SMEs who work in an office environment might be quite comfortable with this arrangement, SMEs who work in the field and rarely have access to an office, computer, or headset will struggle to participate in any meaningful way. I have also seen situations where SMEs often work in underground locations, such as the subway, and can't get reliable Internet access under any circumstances. Unless you find a way to make this work, you risk losing a valuable asset in your project. In this situation, I have seen tablets and headsets purchased for SMEs to allow them to participate while in the field. It is sometimes optional for these field-bound SMEs to visit an office and work from there when necessary. In either case, you need to find a working alternative.

An instructional designer and SMEs work to resolve a content issue.

File sharing is another technological issue that can frustrate everyone involved. There are numerous file-sharing software options available, either in a cloud-based application or something that resides on a server in a specific location. These all require some degree of technical knowledge and the ability to access and load software or apps.

If this is the case for your project, make sure you have each member trained on the use of the products, and be ready to have some level of tech support available, either through the vendor or software publisher. It is a possibility that accessing any files external to a specific network or location where an SME works is not allowed by firewalls and other security precautions. Or, a program may not be available in the operating system used by a particular SME.

It is often the case with technological issues that SMEs have better, more reliable technology in their homes than they do at work. This brings issues of overtime into play and asking someone to spend personal time on project-related activities. There is also the possibility that an SME will ask for reimbursement for Internet access, or the use of their computer and related equipment. These are all issues to be addressed and you should find compromises that work for everyone involved.

The last issue with technology that I have seen happen on occasion is the necessity of purchasing specialized software or hardware for some aspect of a project. This can be many types of software, ranging from a basic word-processing program, to incredibly expensive specialized software to create deliverables. Hardware can range from printers and scanners to workplace health and safety gear that needs to be part of a curriculum, but that no one has yet purchased. There are times when SMEs want to purchase these items and be reimbursed. The issue then turns into who owns the software and hardware, and has access to it during and after the project.

You may have to develop a policy on these issues, which will be influenced by any regulations relating to purchase and ownership associated with grants and other funding sources. No matter what you decide, everyone will probably expect the same treatment when it comes to these expenditures. Providing for one may mean providing for all.

Deadlocked Committees

It is not unusual that opinions will differ on content issues during the process of working with SMEs. These are often easily resolved, and are often just a matter of clarification. There are, however, times when committees have trouble coming to consensus on key content issues.

Sometimes these differences are legitimate content issues, such as deciding which processes or skills are to be included in a course. At other times, they are more political and revolve around issues not specifically related to content, but associated with questions like which title or organization should be performing specific work at specific locations.

There are times when resolving this issue is best left to the committee itself to work through and find a solution. When this approach fails, it often falls back on the training team leadership to try and facilitate a compromise. In worst-case scenarios, I have seen this issue passed to the board or management team. In labor management situations, this sometimes includes negotiations and formal written agreements, but these situations are extremely rare among committee members.

In all cases, don't allow committee deadlocks to become personal and change the scope of the relationship you have with your SMEs.

In all cases, don't allow these issues to become personal and change the scope of the relationship you have with your SMEs. Generally these are resolved quickly and things get back on track without further problems.

Personality Conflicts

We have all experienced this phenomenon in our professional life, and unfortunately there are times when people just don't get along very well. SMEs are no different, especially given the egos involved in trying to assert content knowledge in a very competitive and accomplished group. Having a personality-based problem like this in your SME committee can be a very tricky situation to resolve.

In my experience, personality conflicts are often based on past experiences between several SMEs that can't be left at the door. Whether these are legitimate grievances or just childish behavior, they still need to be fixed one way or another. You always hope that adults will eventually talk out any issues and move on, but this isn't always the case with deeply held resentment, or even stronger emotions between two or more of your team members.

If there are only two SMEs with a problem, you may want to first try to separate them from the group and attempt to facilitate an understanding that will get you through the project. This often works, and they either solve their differences or at least agree to ignore them for the duration of their work together. In extreme cases you may have to remove one or both from the project.

If you have groups of SMEs who refuse to get along, stronger measures may be necessary. I have seen factional differences escalate to total chaos in a few committees, but this is the extreme exception. Usually you can negotiate a truce during committee work sessions that negates any disruption of your project. If no compromise can be found, there may need to be an escalation of the problem to a level where substantive discussions and options can be implemented.

Usually you can negotiate a truce during committee work sessions that negates any disruption of your project.

The biggest mistake you can make when personalities enter the picture is to allow it to fester until it becomes much more difficult to mediate. In many cases time will heal the initial feelings and progress can be made. If not, act quickly and decisively without taking sides or expressing an opinion.

Outside Interference or Interests

Outside work or interests can interfere with work done on the content of your project. This takes several forms, including directed participation by someone who is tangentially associated with the project. It can also involve outside interests that directly benefit a particular SME or organization.

In the case of outside direction for participation, you might notice that an SME has to constantly check with another person not working in the group for clarification or permission on content elements. Numerous phone calls, emails, or text messages can take place while everyone else is on hold. This quickly becomes a problem that needs to be addressed. Possible remedies include replacing the SME with someone who has the authority to make decisions, or having a discussion with the SME and requesting clarification on why this keeps happening.

When outside or consulting business interests are attempting to influence your discussions, you will see one or more SMEs constantly trying to steer work toward themselves or a related outside organization. This can include project-related work, either instructional design or printing, coding, and so on. You may also see pressure to use certain brands of equipment related to the content. These brands could either be in use or are being considered for use, and will directly benefit the SME or his organization if chosen. The degree to which this is obvious and troubling depends on the situation and the expectations of the group and project. I have seen times when SMEs were removed from a project because they ended up being salespeople and not contributing members of the SME team. There are times when original equipment manufacturers (OEM) are vital to your project, and this takes place and is accepted in its own practices.

Conclusion

While there are numerous issues that can impact your SME committees, there are very productive ways to get things back on track if anything happens.

Discussion Questions

1. At what point do you think it is better to facilitate an issue involving personality conflicts in an SME committee? Should you ever get involved?

2. It is becoming obvious to you that one of your SMEs is trying to generate work for her company through her participation on the committee. What, if anything, should you do about this issue?

3. Is there ever a time when it is best to let an SME committee work out its issues without your intervention?

 ## Case Study Question

A usually very efficient and collegial SME committee has suddenly found itself having a major disagreement over a decision about what content to include in a module. While it hasn't become personal or unprofessional, it is obvious there is tension in the committee and the group is not getting any closer to making decisions. What should you do as a project manager to facilitate a compromising solution? Is there any time when you shouldn't get involved in trying to move the group to consensus on these decisions?

Chapter 9

ISD Boot Camp for SMEs

Chapter Objectives

At the end of chapter 9, you will be able to:

- Determine appropriate content to teach SMEs about ISD.
- Outline the content for an ISD boot camp course.
- Provide answers for common questions you may receive from SMEs.
- Design a list of ISD terms to share with SMEs.

Chapter Overview

Providing SMEs an overall view of the instructional design process will lead to a strong foundation for your project. Even a small amount of information allows for a better understanding of your work and priorities, and opens the door for a greater working relationship between the training team and the SMEs.

Why Take Time to Teach SMEs ISD?

To the uninitiated SME, the detail and complexity of the work performed in training and instructional design has the appearance of being way more complicated than necessary. All of our interest in objectives, sequencing, performance standards, and myriad other details just seems unnecessary for the task at hand. Why can't we just "teach them this stuff" and move on?

Part of the misunderstanding comes from the fact that very little is actually known about instructional design and developing training outside the small circle of design professionals. Most SMEs are much more familiar with the legacy design practices of making an outline on a piece of paper and teaching from notes, or lecturing for an hour and asking for questions. Distance and online learning join social media as just "crazy talk" and don't really affect most SMEs. They come by this feeling honestly, and this is another example of the vacuum of information that exists concerning professional curriculum design.

The discussion of why this is the case could fill yet another book, but the fact remains that very few SMEs understand what we do and why we do it. And to be honest, why should they care? If we rely on them for content information, isn't it fair to assume that they should rely on us for the training magic? As experienced designers know, we always learn some of the content while working on a project because most SMEs are very generous with their knowledge if you show some interest in their work. Why not return the favor and share some basic ISD information to assist in their understanding of our side of the work?

Simplifying the Process

Often, SMEs feel they have to provide more than just content knowledge to the process. Sometimes they are overly helpful in writing objectives and other basic design tasks when they feel like there is a vacuum in the process they are trying to fill. This may come from a lack of confidence in the design team or simply a misconception about their role on the team.

It seems logical that a little time spent in an overview of the curriculum design process would improve both understanding and appreciation, and lead to a more efficient and productive relationship between SMEs and designers.

At this point in the process of working with SMEs, it becomes useful and productive to hold a boot camp covering ISD basics. This is almost always time well spent and offers advantages to everyone involved in the instructional design process. Don't forget that instructional designers and trainers are SMEs, too, and sharing some of this knowledge and experience really helps build a committee.

A group of instructional designers and SMEs reviewing the ISD process.

Trainers sometimes assume that SMEs don't care about the curriculum design process and this is a mistake. Most do. Think about it this way: In the process of working with designers, SMEs recognize that questions are asked in specific ways and that we put emphasis on certain aspects of their knowledge. They know we have a process and want certain information from them in specific ways. This curiosity opens the door to making them a more informed and useful participant in the process.

The subtle points related to writing performance-based objectives, sequencing from simple to complex, and deciding evaluative measurement standards are key to design. The more information our SMEs know about the process, the better they are able to support and enhance the process and the final product. The unexpected outcome of sharing process information is efficiency. An informed SME is an efficient and directed member of your team who is more than willing to mold his input to fit your needs.

It is also true that most trainers and instructional designers were first SMEs, and this may be their inaugural exposure to instructional design in a professional setting. This process is very detailed and is based on a systems approach to the work, which interests many professionals, and the more you can offer insights into how it all works, the more beneficial it is to the process.

Timing

While each SME and committee is different, there are at least two windows of opportunity in the process where offering specific ISD information is productive. In the beginning of a project—before any work has been performed—is a good time to provide ISD instruction. Also, at the start of specific process points is helpful, such as analysis, when creating objectives, or when deciding on evaluation tasks or instruments. Of course, each situation is different, but this theme is fairly consistent.

You want to provide a framework for not only how a process works, but also why. It isn't good enough to simply say that you are going to be using instructional design to gather information. SMEs deserve to know not only what instructional design means as it relates to their work, but also how all of the pieces of the process work together, and why their input and support is vital to success.

What to Teach First-Time SMEs

The timing of your training has a lot to do with what you want to cover. Too much information in the beginning of working together may be confusing, and it may be a real turn-off for some if it is overly technical. Striking the right balance depends on several factors.

First, you want to know if this is the first time an SME has worked in the training environment in any capacity. Many SMEs have been used as trainers, guest speakers, or in hundreds of nondesign roles. Others may have varied experience levels with some aspect of curriculum design. In almost all cases, there is limited and perhaps distorted knowledge of instructional design as a professional endeavor.

Where to Start?

Ask yourself the following question: "What are the three elements of ISD that I want each of my SMEs to know while working on a project with me?" Each of us will answer this differently, but there is probably a resonating theme in the elements of ISD that we want to share and make common knowledge in our learning community.

One sure way to answer this question is to review what you are asking your SMEs to supply you in the design process. If you are working to write objectives, the obvious first thing to share with your SMEs is why and how you write objectives and what you actually use them for in the final design product. Other common SME activities are writing evaluations and sequencing learning modules, both of which are simple ISD concepts that can be shared with SMEs in less than an hour.

A Simple One-Hour ISD Boot Camp Overview

Taking 60 minutes to provide an overview of the ISD process and the role of the trainer and designer in the process will pay huge dividends further in your work with SMEs. It doesn't have to be complicated, and usually works best if it isn't. Consider using handouts to supplement your presentation. The ASTD *Infoline* "Teach SMEs to Design Training" or the *Infoline* "Basics of ISD Revisited" work nicely if you have the time to get copies. There are also books from ASTD that cover the topic more thoroughly, including *ISD From the Ground Up*.

The depth to which you prepare this course is up to you. The more it resembles the work you will produce in your project with your SMEs, however, the more the concepts will hit home and stand as an example for them to review.

> **The more your ISD boot camp resembles the work you will produce in your project with your SMEs, however, the more the concepts will hit home and stand as an example for them to review.**

Boot Camp Objectives

Given handouts, discussions, and projected media, the ISD boot-camp participant should be able to:

- Define the term *instructional systems development*.
- List the five elements of the ADDIE model of ISD.
- Name the four parts of a behavioral objective.
- List the four types of evaluation.
- List the responsibilities of the SMEs.
- List the responsibilities of the design team.

> ### *Boot Camp Schedule*
>
> 00:00 to 00:10—ISD definition
>
> 00:11 to 00:20—ADDIE
>
> 00:21 to 00:30—Objectives
>
> 00:31 to 00:40—Evaluation
>
> 00:41 to 00:50—SME roles
>
> 00:51 to 01:00—Design team roles
>
> This is a really tight schedule and can easily be expanded to meet your needs and available time. While two or more hours would be nice, it isn't always possible or necessary early in the project. You can always expand later as necessary and provide more detail as requested.

Questions You Are Likely to Receive From SMEs

If you decide not to have a boot camp or other overview for your SMEs, you should review this list of common questions with them so that you at least open the door to more in-depth discussion as necessary.

After years of working with SMEs on committees and hundreds of projects, I have noticed there is a core set of questions this really smart group of people repeatedly asks. They want to know about instructional design and what happens on the other side of the table. This is a great place to start in terms of thinking about what you want to share with your content experts. I have provided short answers for each question to give you a start on how to approach answers for your group.

Q: What is ISD?

A: ISD stands for instructional systems development, and it is a systems approach to developing courses. It has five basic elements that include analysis, design, development, implementation, and evaluation.

Q: What are objectives and why do we spend so much time working on them?

A: Objectives represent the content that we will expect each student to be able to master at the end of each course or module. They are divided into four parts: audience, behavior, condition, and degree. We spend so much time writing objectives because they are the key to providing a roadmap for both our students and for our instructors when we implement a course. Objectives are written in this much detail because it takes this much data to make sure that students are able to reach mastery. Objectives also assist in sequencing, and allow us to make sure we cover all of the important content and are not missing anything vital to student success.

Q: What is the difference between goals and objectives?

A: Goals are generalized objectives. Goals might include "increasing sales" or "explaining the new vacation policy." Objectives are specific behaviors that are both observable and measurable, and can be evaluated.

Q: Are there different types of evaluation?

A: Evaluation is divided into four different types based on the work of Donald Kirkpatrick and Jack and Patti Phillips. You may hear of these as Kirkpatrick's four levels of evaluation, even though they are not actually levels and you don't have to do one before the others. In fact, most evaluation on one project is done with just one or two of these types.

The four types of evaluation are

- reaction

- learning

- behavior

- return-on-investment.

You are probably most familiar with reaction evaluations, which are commonly called "smile sheets." Reaction evaluation looks at the way a student responded to a learning experience. They have little information relating to mastery of content—except an occasional self-evaluation—and are more focused on the learning environment and how well they liked the course and surroundings.

Learning evaluations measure the mastery of the content of a course based on an objective process like a quiz, test, case study, role play, or observation. Objectives are the key element in these evaluations, since you are determining whether a student can meet the objectives as described in the course.

When we look at the impact a course had on a student after implementation, we use a behavior evaluation. This is a look at how much—if any—of the content was actually used by the student at an interval of three months or more after they took the course. These evaluations will tell us if there was any impact of the course over the long term.

> **Behavior evaluation is a look at how much—if any—of the content was actually used by the student at an interval of three months or more after they took the course.**

Return-on-investment evaluations, often called ROI, are usually thought of in terms of monetary measurement, but in reality they are an evaluation of what was gained or lost in any important measurement as the result of a course. While elements like increased sales or productivity are one measure with ROI, you can also look at morale, reduced sick time, or any factor that relates directly to the course content as measured after the course is offered.

Q: How does someone become an instructional designer?

A: There are as many answers to this question as there are instructional designers, but there are some basic paths to take. Most instructional designers started as something else, either as an SME, teacher, trainer, or as a training or human resources professional. There are a growing number of people who choose ISD as a career, and study the process through course offerings from the American Society for Training & Development (ASTD) or other organizations. ASTD offers a Certified Professional in Learning and Performance (CPLP) certification, which has become an industry standard for instructional designers.

Academic programs are available at the University of Maryland Baltimore County (UMBC), which offers both a master's degree in ISD and graduate certificates in ISD, instructional technology, and distance learning. Other excellent colleges and universities also offer credit courses and degrees in ISD and other related fields.

Q: Why does the instructor's guide contain so much information?

A: Instructor's guides are the handbook for how to teach a course. They contain several sections which all work together to successfully implement a course. Even short courses that last an hour or less get the same level of detail.

The basic sections of an instructor's guide include pre-class information, a detailed guide to teaching the course, and a final evaluation section. The pre-class section details what materials and equipment are needed to teach the course, as well as a checklist of items to do before the course starts.

The instructor's guide or lesson plan (as it is often called in ISD), is actually a step-by-step approach to teaching the course. It is modeled after the work of Robert Gagne and can contain as many as nine separate sections for each block of a course. Instructional designers call these the nine events of instruction, and they reflect the way students process and learn content in a course. Many times there will be less than nine actual steps depending on the course and delivery method.

The final element of the instructor's guide is the evaluation section, and it contains any content-related evaluation instruments like quizzes and tests, as well as any process evaluation instruments like a reaction evaluation or smile sheet.

Q: You folks use a lot of jargon; what does some of it mean?

A: Instructional design is full of jargon, acronyms, and just plain gibberish. Here are some of the most commonly used terms.

ISD—can mean either instructional systems development or instructional systems design.

SME—a subject matter expert, sometimes pronounced "smeeeeeee."

ADDIE—this is the generic or basic model of instructional design, and includes the elements of A-analysis, D-design, D-development, I-implementation and E-evaluation.

ABCD Objectives—in most applications, behavioral objectives have four parts which are A-audience, B-behavior, C-condition, and D-degree. These are also referred to as four-part objectives.

9 Events or Gagne's 9 Events—this refers to a lesson plan format that uses nine separate learning events as the basis for how it is written. It was originally developed by Robert Gagne of Florida State University in the 1970s. The nine events are

1. gaining attention
2. direction
3. recall
4. content
5. application-feedback level one
6. application-feedback level two
7. application-feedback level three

8. evaluation

9. closure.

Level 1 evaluation—this refers to Kirkpatrick's work on evaluation and level one. While not really a level at all, it refers to a simple reaction or smile-sheet evaluation.

Level 2 evaluation—this refers to the second of Kirkpatrick's four types of evaluation, and this measures learning.

Level 3 evaluation—Kirkpatrick's third type of evaluation is a behavioral evaluation, and it measures whether a course has had any impact on a student after a set time, usually at least three months out.

ROI—this is Jack and Patti Phillips' type of evaluation and refers to return-on-investment for a course or program within instructional design.

LMS—stands for learning management system, and it is the interface used in online learning between the software and the students and instructors.

Synchronous—the term used when online learners (or any learners for that matter) are online at the same time participating in a course.

Asynchronous—this is when online students access a course at different times, with no expectation of interacting with other students or the instructor.

Q: What are learner and facilitator prerequisites?

A: Prerequisites are the criteria or minimum standards expected for both students and facilitators to either participate in or teach a course. Prerequisites for students can include the completion of a previous course, a specific grade level, or other criteria. Prerequisites for a facilitator might include a specific level of education or certification, years of experience, language skills, or other expectations.

How Much Is Too Much?

At some point the amount of ISD information given at one time can be overwhelming and enough quickly becomes too much. Pacing and keeping up a dialogue about ISD and the process works best at determining what to offer and when.

Always be open to the signs that indicate whether more information is wanted. Expanding incrementally is usually the best practice.

Conclusion

Providing your SMEs with the basics of ISD is a great idea in almost any environment. The timing and amount of this information is something that is different for each group, but starting with the basics early in a project and following up with more detailed information later as the process matures is a good model to follow.

Discussion Questions

1. What do you think is the best information about ISD to share with an SME early in a project?

2. Is there ever a point where providing too much information about ISD is a bad idea?

3. Would you ever consider having an SME work on the design team in a non-content role?

 ## Case Study Question

You are working with an SME who is showing a lot of interest in working in instructional design, but insists that ISD is mostly just "smoke and mirrors" and that you don't need all of this detail or effort to design training. How would you approach this attitude in an SME?

Chapter 10

Migrating SMEs Into Mainstream Training and ISD Roles

Chapter Objectives

At the end of chapter 10, you will be able to:

- Determine the best way to begin the integrations of SMEs into training roles.
- Suggest and apply solutions for transitional resistance in SMEs.

Chapter Overview

There are many SMEs who would like to become more active in traditional training and instructional design roles. Having a plan for assisting this talented group of professionals goes a long way toward building this relationship.

The migration of SMEs—especially technical, hybrid, and instructional—to the roles of trainers and instructional designers is now so common that it is an accepted part of many organizations' planning. It is fair to say before the professionalization of training and ISD starting in the late 1970s, most large training departments were primarily staffed by SMEs moving from the ranks into these positions. This was especially true in manufacturing, transportation, utilities, the military, and other similar fields.

The reasons for this vary, but it was commonly seen as good practice to move the best performers on the job into training. The feeling was that the best worker is probably the best person to train others, and there are certainly examples of that. While often lacking in formal education in training or instructional design, they know instinctively what to teach and what is important to share with younger, less experienced workers.

In the professional ranks of business, finance, engineering, law, and medicine, the traditional journey through the academic system supported training approaches that in some ways mimicked the academic environment. They were more likely to have training departments staffed and managed by career trainers and designers. Even in these organizational cultures, the best performers were asked to participate in training programs and projects that benefitted from their experience.

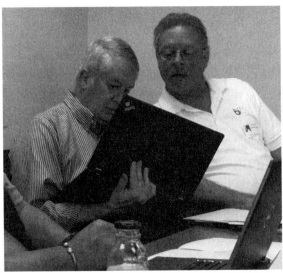

Two SMEs discussing the best way to design a technical course for apprentices.

The graying of the population of Baby Boomers and the post-World War II generation leaves many experienced employees in a position where they are unable to continue to work in physically demanding occupational titles, but are too valuable to their organizations not to be employed to best advantage. There are also employees who just want to try something new and get out of their day-to-day grind on the job. They want to share their knowledge with others as trainers and course designers.

There is also an active group of highly skilled workers who see an opportunity in training that interests them, and they would like to make a career move to enter either training or instructional design.

Regardless of how any of these talented individuals arrive in training departments, they are all SMEs, and there is a need to bring them up to speed in the fields of adult learning, instructional design, and now the world of online and mobile learning.

Within every population of content experts, you will find an interest in learning more about what you do. One day, they might want to join you.

Getting Started

To many SMEs, the practice of instructional design and the training world in general sometimes seems like overly detailed busy work when seen from the outside. The excruciating detail and jargon alone are enough to send some of them packing. Often the first time they hear themselves called "smeeezs" they feel patronized or worse.

Early on in the process of bringing along content experts, it is necessary to humanize the practice of instructional design, plus present it as a legitimate field of practice that is both art and science. Most probably don't realize that graduate degrees in instructional design even exist, or that many of the new crop of trainers and designers have never held line or staff functions in any other field.

It is also important to point out that many trainers and designers have come from the ranks of SMEs, and the path to a career in the field can be both academic and context-expert based. While a degree or certificate is something that might be of interest, it isn't required in many training positions.

First ISD Roles

The first move from SME to ISD can be something simple, like working on writing objectives or sequencing a set of objectives—anything that allows a content expert to have some ownership of the process. I have often seen an interest in preparing draft lesson plans, or working on the production of project media or handouts. While these may seem like elementary tasks in the larger scheme of a project, it is these types of activities that build interest and confidence.

Another important aspect of this early work is to make sure that your new designers get lots of feedback and the backstory on why something is done and how it relates to the larger picture. This insider information is important; it allows for questions and discussions relating to the work within a project.

Providing Background Information

Early on in this process, you should provide either an entry-level ISD book or an ASTD *Infoline* on ISD or some aspect of training. This reinforces the work you are doing with your SMEs. It is something they can review on their own time and reference later as their involvement grows. If you have a large enough group, you should consider a 20-hour overview of ISD, with lots of hands-on exercises taken directly from the work going on within the organization—sort of an informal internal internship.

The ISD boot camp course discussed in chapter 9 might prove to be an excellent way to get started with this group. If they have already taken the course or something similar, try to determine the areas that you might find useful to have them working in at this point of their involvement. It also works well to ask them what interests them and determine if there is a fit for their interest and your present needs.

Transitional Resistance

In many SMEs who turn to training and instructional design, I have found that they often have a very rigid viewpoint on what they think works and is necessary in curriculum development. Often this includes a tendency to oversimplify. They don't appreciate the need for detail that seasoned instructional designers have found to be necessary. This may include a resistance to formal objectives and evaluation tasks. You may also discover that this group finds nothing wrong with seminars and webinars as training vehicles, even though there are no objectives or evaluations attached.

You may also discover that this group finds nothing wrong with seminars and webinars as training vehicles, even though there are no objectives or evaluations attached.

This naïveté is not borne of laziness or lack of willingness to engage in the hard work involved in course design. Often its genesis is in the fact that much of the design process is not obvious to either learners or instructors unless they have been involved in the design process themselves. The best example is the building of a home. It looks rather simple and uncomplicated until you dig into the blueprints and run up against your first unexpected challenge, such as choosing the wrong materials or not meeting building codes. The most experienced building trade workers will always caution against trivializing the complexity of the building process. Same for our work as trainers and instructional designers.

When working with this transitional group, be sure to have the patience to discuss and provide examples for all of the concepts that you forward concerning course design. I have found it useful to provide examples of what worked well and what didn't work so well as teaching points in the process. These real-world discussions go a long way in providing the openings for productive conversations about objectives, evaluations, delivery methods, and documentation of mastery.

Interest Group Approach

There are times when initiating an ISD interest group in your organization can provide the entry point for SMEs interested in learning more about training and instructional design. This can be a lunch-and-learn format, or even a discussion board on the organization's website that solicits questions and provides background information for anyone interested in the topic.

You might want to consider holding an optional after-work overview of ISD that might catch the interest of SMEs whom you have worked with in the past. This could also be jointly hosted by human resources if you have a pool of redundant employees looking for a new skill. In this scenario you want to make sure you have potential work they could participate in. Don't just offer an overview without any real prospect of working on a project.

◇◇

Conclusion

Providing a path for interested SMEs to join the training family pays dividends for all involved. This doesn't, however, happen by accident. You need to have a plan for making sure that SMEs learn what is important for your work. Make sure they get opportunities to learn about instructional design and how to use new skills in areas they find interesting.

◇◇

Discussion Questions

1. What attributes and skills do you think are most important when assessing if an SME has potential as a trainer or instructional designer?

2. Do you think the best SME always makes the best trainer? Why?

3. How did you first learn about ISD and did anyone offer you any assistance or information to get started? Did you start as an SME?

Case Study Question

You have just completed a year-long project with 10 SMEs, and several of them have mentioned learning more about ISD and perhaps working on a future project as a trainer. You know from experience that several of them have very strong views on instructional design, and have mentioned that ISD is really just common sense and that you don't need to go to all that effort to get the same results. How would you handle this as a project manager?

Chapter 11

SME Dos and Don'ts

Chapter Objectives

At the end of chapter 11, you will be able to:

- List things you should always do when working with your SMEs.
- List things you must never do when working with your SMEs.

Chapter Overview

Years of experience have garnered a long list of the best ways to work with SMEs. Experience has also provided the equally long list of things to never do with your SMEs. It is always helpful to look at what the training and instructional design pros think about working with their SMEs.

We have covered a lot of different aspects of working with content experts, and now it is time to hear from instructional designers and trainers about their experiences with SMEs. I have asked numerous very experienced professionals to offer what they think should be on the ultimate list of dos and don'ts when working with SMEs.

This is not a complete list and not every suggestion will work in all situations, but this is a powerful list of what works and doesn't work from experiences over many years of frontline work in ISD with SMEs. This isn't exactly a best-practices list, since

I think working with SMEs is a much more detailed endeavor than something that warrants only a generalized best-practices approach.

These are not in order of importance, and are meant to serve as ideas for you to consider in your work. You should add your own items as you gain experience working with SMEs.

Things You Must Always Do When Working With SMEs

- Show appreciation for the time and effort your SMEs invest in your project.
- Acknowledge their content expertise.
- Take the time to really know your SMEs' strengths and weaknesses.
- Always provide clear guidelines on their roles and your expectations.
- Be attentive and responsive to SME concerns.
- Be as flexible as possible while realizing SMEs have busy professional lives outside your project.
- Always seek their review and comments.
- Make sure every SME has a chance to participate in discussions and meetings.
- Always provide copies of finished products and projects.
- Celebrate milestones and victories with your SMEs.

Let's look at these one at a time and explore why they are so important. Remember that this list came from a seasoned group of trainers and instructional designers with a combined experience of well over a hundred years. Sometimes these are obvious and easy to implement, but other times they take some thought and a little work to pull off successfully.

Show Appreciation

This isn't something specific to working with SMEs or even related only to professional relationships, but it is one of the most basic tenets of associating successfully with other people. Taking the time to let your SMEs know that their time and participation is appreciated will soothe and heal many bumps in the road.

The primary reason this is so important with our SMEs is because they might already feel like an outsider or fifth wheel in the process, and they need that little extra attention to know they are appreciated.

Appreciation can be shown in numerous ways, but the most effective and sincere method is simply saying "thanks" on lots of occasions. You can also provide snacks and beverages at meetings, and send a group email expressing appreciation. Many times it doesn't matter how you do this—it is the fact that you did anything that will make a difference in your relationship with your content experts.

The other important aspect of appreciation is to do it from the beginning of your relationship with your SMEs. Don't wait for the first deadline or milestone; start at the first contact.

Best advice: Be sincere, start immediately, and do it often when working with your SMEs.

Acknowledge Content Expertise

SMEs are very proud of their accomplishments and content knowledge. Every person in this group has worked very hard to get where they are in their careers, and accepting the role of SME in your project often means more to them than they may let on.

There are many opportunities to acknowledge their expertise and provide a little sincere recognition for their work. The success of your work may well rest in their hands, and letting them know that you appreciate what they bring to the process makes a difference to them—sometimes a very big difference.

Sharing an honest curiosity about their work and the content is a genuine method of engaging your SMEs in their comfort zone apart from the design process environment.

Best advice: Express a genuine interest in your SME's work and acknowledge her content knowledge.

Get to Know Them

How many times has a stereotype failed to live up to its reputation in your experience? One area where this becomes a startling reality is when you first begin working with SMEs. While there is always an exception, working with these professionals is many times a lot of fun.

They are smart, confident, and often have a biting sense of humor, especially among themselves. When the design team is allowed into their confidence, it can really open a new door into your perceptions of how this group thinks.

I have often shared many stories about my family and my work experiences that paralleled those of my SMEs when they shared the same with me. The more we shared, the more we realized that we had in common. Sometimes a commonality is where we live, or our high school or college connections. Other times it was just a shared sports interest or vacation experience.

The more you get to know them, the more you realize that they are no different from any group you work with or that lives in your neighborhood. You can't force this relationship, but you can open the door to some degree of personalization within your group. Not everyone cares or participates, but most will if they feel comfortable. This is one area where too much personal information is unprofessional, and no one wants to open the door to unnecessary drama.

> **Best advice:** Take time to get to know each person in the SME family, and don't be afraid to share something of your life and interests in the process.

Be Clear and Concise

This is an obvious requirement in any professional relationship, but with SMEs this takes on added meaning because there is always the opportunity for confusion or misunderstanding about many issues during a project—especially in the beginning.

Make sure that all communication is to the point concerning detail, expectations, due dates, meeting times, and so on. Allow ample opportunity for questions and clarification, and don't be impatient with questions that seem obvious to you.

> **Best advice:** Always take time to communicate in a way that leaves no room for confusion between you and your SMEs.

Be Attentive and Responsive

Managing a project with SMEs requires that you constantly have your listening skills honed to pick up the most subtle concerns, critiques, and requests from your professionals. In the military, requests from officers are met with the reply "I'll take care of that immediately," and working with your SMEs should elicit the same response from you and your team.

Even somewhat obscure or frankly silly requests should be acknowledged and some response given. In these situations, it is silence that causes the most harm.

Best advice: Always listen and respond immediately to your SMEs.

Be Flexible

Schedules and deliverables are usually the biggest sources of conflict when working with SMEs on a project. Your desired schedule and expectations are sometimes not realistic to your SMEs for multiple reasons.

Even after protracted discussions and negotiations, it is sometimes impossible for someone to meet a deadline, and being flexible in these situations will pay dividends. This isn't to say that chronic problems don't exist (and those need to be addressed differently), but the usual ebb and flow in this process needs to take place, and the less stress on everyone, the better the result.

Best advice: Find compromise and be open to changes as situations warrant with your SMEs.

Seek Their Review and Comments

The philosophy of some trainers and instructional designers is that SMEs are best used for information and then essentially forgotten later in the project. This is a losing proposition.

SMEs generally appreciate being part of the review and revisions process. And, the best part of including them is that they always have good ideas, and they are the best people to find errors in content. As with any group, there is a point at which you need to finish, but one round of review and comments is worth the time and effort. This can be accomplished either in person, by conferencing, or even by sending along copies for comment to each SME.

One area that pays large dividends is when you need to prioritize content and make decisions about what to use and what to ignore in the content. This generally happens later in the process, and this will require a specific request and follow-up as necessary.

> **Best advice:** Always include your SMEs in the review and comment process.

Equalize Participation

Just like with any group of people, the introverts and the extroverts have different ways of communicating, and SMEs are no different. While some will dominate discussions, others will sit back in silence until asked to participate.

I have seen many really quiet SMEs provide project-changing input only after being asked to participate. If left to participate on their own, they would have never spoken up or become part of the conversation.

There are many ways to see that this happens, and you will just need to make sure that everyone has equal opportunities to speak, discuss, and participate. Don't let anyone just sit silently by during these important meetings.

> **Best advice:** Make it standard practice to see that everyone participates at every level, and that every SME has a say.

Provide Finished Copies

Nothing says success better than a product in hand that everyone is proud of. SMEs are as proud of their work as any other professional, and a copy of a finished course sitting on a bookshelf proudly displayed for everyone to see sends a strong message about participation.

Everyone who works on a project should have at least one copy of the finished product. SMEs should always get a copy of at least one module or course for others to see and appreciate. While a complete set of materials for everyone is probably not practical, at least see that your SMEs get a copy of the portion of the course they worked on in recognition of their contributions. I have many times asked the design team to sign and inscribe a message of appreciation to each SME before they are distributed.

> **Best advice:** Share a copy of the finished product so that your SMEs can be proud of their contributions to the success of the project.

Celebrate

I doubt any of you need a reason to celebrate a successful project or a milestone in course development, but many times the SMEs are not part of the event. For more reasons than need to be listed, always incorporate your SMEs in celebrations and acknowledgments.

I always encourage groups to have a special lunch or dinner where everyone can gather together informally and reflect on the work that a group of SMEs has accomplished. It is also a nice touch to have certificates or other form of appreciation to distribute to everyone who participated. At some of these gatherings, every SME and team member has a chance to say something about their work with the group, and these are very often incredibly powerful motivational events for everyone involved. It is a pleasant surprise to hear so many positive comments about the process and the people working on the project.

Best advice: Never fail to celebrate milestones and deadlines with your SME groups.

Things You Must Never Do When Working With SMEs

- Fail to make your SMEs part of your design team.
- Ignore or take SME participation for granted.
- Talk in jargon.
- Show impatience.
- Have an opinion relating to content.
- Revisit discussions or decisions already completed.
- Fail to involve all SMEs equally in discussions.
- Miss deadlines.

Never Fail to Make SMEs Part of Your Design Team

The single biggest mistake experienced trainers and instructional designers make with SMEs is failing to make SMEs part of the design team. Treating them as outsiders or as just another element of the process will always work against your success.

There are numerous reasons why this is the case. First, talented professionals have earned the right to have a seat at the table with everyone else. To treat them with any less respect will inject an instant (and probably indelible) negative attitude toward you and the project.

Second, they are very unlikely to give you their best effort without feeling like an integral part of the team. If they feel like an outsider, they will only perform at a minimal level more times than not, and offer little if anything beyond what is perceived as expected.

It is also true that whatever their experience with you, the word will quickly spread that you aren't easy to work with or that you don't appreciate the effort SMEs put into the work. Future SMEs will show up with a negative attitude before you even get started.

Building a team with SMEs also allows for increased efficiency and a real boost to quality in the process and product. These are really smart and motivated professionals who like a challenge and respond well to being appreciated and included. Pretty simple really.

> **Best advice:** From the first moment of contact to the last goodbye, make your SMEs feel like part of the team.

Never Ignore or Take Your SMEs for Granted

The second biggest mistake that trainers and designers make—next to not including SMEs on the team—is taking them for granted or acting as if they really don't exist. This is markedly different from not making them team members, since you have made a personal commitment and contract with your SMEs once they are on the team, which you have not fulfilled. Call it benign neglect or implied arrogance, but the result is the same in that your SME group feels used and unappreciated.

If you treat your SMEs as if their work is expected and just another day in the office, it is likely what you can expect in return. Smart professionals know how to participate at minimal levels and still get through the day and your project without any undue effort. Don't let this happen under your watch.

> **Best advice:** Treat each SME as if she is a regular part of your design and training family at all times.

Don't Use Jargon

ISD and ADDIE require ABCD objectives for level 2 evals during implementation. And so on…

Every professional endeavor has jargon, acronyms, and other forms of communication torture that outsiders are forced to endure and can only attempt to decipher. For your SMEs, it would be easier to decode your DNA than the jargon you use every day in your work.

It pays to prepare a list of jargon and acronyms that you use in your work and share it with your SMEs. This not only opens the door for them to understand your language and work, it also allows you to work with them to decipher their jargon and acronyms as you build courses. The connection between opening up your world to them and for them to help you is an important link in the curriculum design process, and in building your team.

Best advice: Break the language barrier early with your SMEs and bring them into the training and ISD jargon-sphere.

Don't Be Impatient

There are a very small number of trainers and designers who treat their SMEs as if they were children and often become impatient and grumpy (nicer word choice) with each new question or change in ideas about the content. This attitude can provide a one-way street effect in terms of ever getting any additional work out of your SMEs.

Since the process of ISD is very detailed at times, we sometimes as designers lose track of the fact that outsiders don't have any feel for what we do—especially when they first start working with us. The inevitable questions about what we are doing and why we do things a certain way can sometimes grate on a trainer or instructional designer, and our first instinct is to react negatively to the inquiry. Don't. This is the time to take a break in the process, explain in the necessary detail what is going on, and answer questions. This can be avoided by having a short ISD boot camp (earlier chapter), but there are always additional questions.

The irony of this entire situation is that as trainers and instructional designers we are constantly asking our SMEs to explain what they do in great detail, and if they showed the same level of frustration with us, we would likely get nowhere in our work.

> **Best advice:** Always go the extra mile in being patient with your SMEs.

Don't Get Involved in the Content

Seasoned trainers and instructional designers know when to get involved in content discussion and when to stay as far away as possible. The general rule is that discussions that are only related to fleshing out content are only to be facilitated. At no time should anyone but the SMEs provide content information.

By the same token, as a facilitator, the trainer and instructional designer must make sure that the level of detail and accuracy of the content is confirmed. This can be as easy as having everyone reach consensus on important content discussions. It is also expected that a facilitator will draw out content discussions to make sure that no steps or levels of complexity are missed or ignored. This is especially true when working on sequencing of content.

> **Best advice:** When working on content issues with your SMEs, remain neutral and facilitate the process, not the content.

Don't Revisit Content Decisions Already Made By the SMEs

One of the most annoying habits trainers display with SMEs in the instructional design process is revisiting decisions already made by the SMEs concerning content, both in terms of what is important and sequencing. This is almost universally seen as a challenge to their professional knowledge and skills.

It is fine for a trainer or instructional designer to ask an SME group if everything important is included, or if they want to revisit any of the content issues. It is not advisable to just dive back into a content discussion that has already taken place, and especially if decisions have already been made. This is sacred ground to this group and they don't like to be second-guessed.

Discussion about clarifying and adding content details are expected and are usually not a problem. However, I have seen trainers and instructional designers revisit content from an earlier discussion that was somewhat difficult to facilitate, because of the wide range of views from the SMEs, and bringing it back up for no logical reason just soured the entire process.

Of course, review of the finished drafts of content is perfectly acceptable and logical in the process, but it needs to be made clear that the SMEs are only reviewing their own work and making sure that the design team captured their intent correctly. Change will then be initiated from the SMEs and not the design team.

> **Best advice:** Leave past content alone once the SMEs have decided and moved on with their work.

Don't Play Favorites

Every member of your SME team, with the exception of a committee chair or chairs—if you have them—should participate equally in all of the work requiring their content knowledge. This is a nice way of saying that it is important to see that every single SME has an opportunity and is encouraged to participate in the process and all discussions equally.

Having no favorites among your SMEs is philosophically the same as a parent having no favorites among his children. There are times when you may not like or appreciate certain aspects of their personalities or actions, but they should all be treated the same regarding the process of building courses and content.

The negatives attached to having favorites are fairly obvious but require clarity for our purposes as trainers and instructional designers. In our design world we rely on the best information we can gather from our SMEs. If the process becomes personal or some feel that one or more of the group are treated differently, you will experience a noticeable drop in participation from the self-perceived outsider SMEs.

While this seems obvious and a general statement of good practice with any group, the reality with SMEs is that you may only get one opportunity to work with them and gather the best information available. If you fail to treat all equally, you had better guess correctly on the best and the brightest in your group of SMEs. Otherwise, you will be stuck with what you get from the rest.

> **Best advice:** Treat each SME equally within your team and project.

Don't Miss Deadlines

I'm not sure how obvious this important element of working with SMEs can be, but it has to be said. Miss deadlines and deliverable schedules with your SMEs, and you will no longer have any right to expect any different from them. Setting an example is key in this relationship-building process.

Your ability to make deadlines is a key credibility factor in your relationship with your SMEs, and they notice if you don't make the grade. It signals that something is wrong and they sense problems before you think they do. They also are unlikely to perform at any reasonable standard if the signals you send them are that late and incomplete work is acceptable, as displayed in your work.

> **Best advice:** Meet deadlines and deliverable schedules and your SMEs will probably do the same.

◇◇

Conclusions

There are numerous very important elements to having a great and productive working relationship with SMEs. Listening to the advice of seasoned trainers and instructional designers offers an array of excellent approaches to building and maintaining these key relationships.

◇◇

Discussion Questions

1. What do you think is the single most important thing to do with SMEs?

2. Do you think there are any things that SMEs are too sensitive about when working on a design project?

3. As an SME, what would you find most important in your relationship with a trainer and instructional designer?

Case Study Question

You are managing a course design project and you are working with five SMEs on a weekly basis to complete the project in a short period of time. You are starting to notice that several people in the group are not as enthusiastic about participating, since they were not invited to a team luncheon hosted by the organization, and only found out later from someone on the team. Do you think this is legitimate behavior, and what would you do about it?

Acknowledgments

I want to acknowledge the countless and invaluable contributions that many instructional designers, subject matter experts, colleagues, friends, and family have made that both spiritually and materially assisted in writing this book.

First in line for my appreciation are the thousands of subject matter experts I have had the pleasure of working with and learning from for so many years. Before I knew you had a collective name I was standing in your shadow and taking it all in. If this book in any way makes you feel appreciated and respected, I have accomplished one of my main goals in this effort.

To my academic partner, the University of Maryland Baltimore County and its faculty and staff, specifically Dr. Greg Williams, Sharese Essien, Deb Petska, Jeannette Campos, Dr. Zane Berge, Keith Curran, Carol Erdman, Todd Marks, Paul Kellerman, Dr. Linda Raudenbush, Dr. Stuart Weinstein, Rafi Ahmad, John Beulow, and Dr. Greg Walsh.

I would like to acknowledge the labor-management apprenticeship community and all of the SMEs that on a daily basis inspire and train the next generation of skilled-trade professionals who perform every imaginable task in our complicated and highly technical world. It continues to be my honor to work with this dedicated group of women and men.

Specifically the efforts of the Transportation Learning Center, including Brian Turner, Jack Clark, Julie Deibel, Joyce Williams, Jim Kinahan, Melissa Huber, Amri Hylton, Yvonne Syphax, John Schiavone, Dr. Pat Greenfield, Dr. Robin Gillespie, Xinge Wang, Liz Waller, Mark Dysart, Tia Brown, and Ron Lewis. To the members of the El/ES CDT group including Mike Rodriquez, Alex Rosmondo, Bobby Mizelle,

Carll Sandsbury, Chuck Neal, Danny Brown, David Lacosse, George Younger, Hiram Nix, Jerome Moore, Philip Newton, Tom Waugh, Ed Laguardia, Colleen May, and Shawn Muhummad.

To my thousands of undergraduate and graduate students who taught me much more than I could ever hope to have taught them. Please never stop asking questions.

To the incredible team at ASTD, specifically Juana Llorens and Heidi Smith for their untiring support, encouragement, and reality checks.

To the IOOK and the Loop Group.

To my immediate support group, including my partner Karen Smith and her children Nick and Savannah Ransom, and to my children Heather, David, and Joe Hodell.

Thanks is never enough.

Chuck Hodell
May, 2013
The Woods
Hedgesville, West Virginia

About the Author

Chuck Hodell is the author of the best-selling ASTD book *ISD From the Ground Up* and has been involved in the worlds of training and education for more than 30 years. He has written extensively on instructional design and training-related topics for ASTD, including several *Infolines*. He has enjoyed stints as a musician, police officer, telephone company repair technician, trainer, teacher, and academic administrator. Like many training professionals, his first exposure to training and instructional design was as an SME, or subject matter expert. He currently serves as associate director of the graduate program in instructional systems development at the University of Maryland Baltimore County. He is also the senior program director for instructional design at the Transportation Learning Center and academic advisor to the International Masonry Institute. Hodell has an undergraduate degree from Antioch University and an MA and PhD from the University of Maryland Baltimore County.

Index

A

ABCD objectives, 113
Academic credentials, 4
Access, 96–97
Acronyms, 113–114, 131
ADDIE model, 5, 12, 53, 113
Appreciation, showing, 124–125
Apprenticeship committees, 38
Areas of expertise, 3
Asynchronous, 114
Attentiveness, 126–127
Availability, 98

B

Baby Boomers, 118
Background information, 120
Background materials, 53
Behavior evaluation, 111–112
Board, 64
Building trades credentials, 4

C

Celebration, 129
Certified Professional in Learning and
    Performance certification, 6, 112
Classroom-based courses, 61
Comments, seeking of, 127
Committee(s)
    apprenticeship, 38
    building of, 32
    considerations for, 39

consolidation of, 33
deadlocked, 100–101
demanding behavior effects on, 87
disagreements in, 100–101
formation of, 34
independent, 35
instructional design support for, 40
leadership of, 40–42, 101
managed, 36, 38
matrix, 36
overview of, 31–32
personality conflicts in, 102
range-of-experience, 37–38
scale of project considerations, 34
scheduling conflicts, 97–98
size of, 38–39
structure of, 35–38
working with, 32–33
Communication
    clarity and conciseness in, 126
    information about, 51
    as performance evaluation criterion, 82
    problems addressed through, 67
    SME selection based on, 21–22
Computer hardware, 100
Conflicts
    personality, 101–102
    scheduling, 97–98
Contact information, 51
Content
    geographic elements that affect, 19
    involvement with, 132
    revisiting of decisions about, 132–133

scope creep with, 65–66
SME decisions about, 132–133
stability of, 18
Content experts
    definition of, 3
    levels of, 37
    number of, on committees, 39
    personal life issues affecting, 67
    support environment for, 41
Content knowledge
    acknowledging of, 125
    depth of, 78–79
    description of, 16
    expectations for, 78–80
    relevance of, 78
    timeliness of, 79–80
Content-related SMEs, 6
Contracts
    costs addressed in, 28
    issues addressed in, 26–27
    time commitment addressed in, 27–28
    workday defined in, 28
Cooperation, 84–85
Copies of finished products, 128
Costs, 28, 100
Course development process, 47–48
CPLP certification. *See* Certified Professional
    in Learning and Performance certification
Credentials, 4

D

Deadlines
    defining of, 63
    importance of, 73–74
    missing, 82, 134
    performance evaluation based on meet-
        ing of, 82
    setting of, 74
Deadlocked committees, 100–101
Decision making
    outside interferences with, 102
    by sentinel SMEs, 64
Deliverables
    deficiency in, 82
    description of, 72–73
    due date for, 81–82

flexibility with, 127
Demanding behavior, 87
Depth of content knowledge, 78–79.
    See Depth of experience
Depth of experience, 18
Design documents, 70
Design team, SME involvement in, 129–130

E

Equipment, 103
Evaluation
    performance, criteria used in. *See*
        Performance evaluation criteria
    types of, 111–112, 114
Expectations, 58, 61, 67
Experience
    depth of, 18
    description of, 3–4
    location of, 19–20
    relevance of, 17
    timeliness of, 18–19
    training/teaching, 20
Expertise
    acknowledging of, 125
    areas of, 3

F

Facilitators
    description of, 62
    prerequisites, 114
Favoritism, 133
Feedback, 119
Field-bound SMEs, 99
File sharing, 99–100
Finished products, 128
First impression, 46–48
First outreach, 50–51
Flexibility, 127
Formula for successful starts. *See* Project start,
    formula for success in
Functional SMEs
    characteristics of, 10
    ISD elements and, 12–13
    roles and responsibilities of, 63–64

G

Gagne's 9 Events, 113–114
General skills criteria, 21–23
Genius factor, 4
Geographic location, 19
Goals, 111

H

Hybrid SMEs
    characteristics of, 9
    ISD elements and, 12–13
    pilot study implementation by, 43
    roles and responsibilities of, 8–9, 60–61
    technical SMEs versus, 61

I

Impatience, 131–132
Inaction, 67
Independent committee, 35
Inflation of role, 66
In-house SMEs, 48, 96
Initial contact, 51
Insecurity, 88
Instructional designer
    academic programs for becoming, 112
    committee supported by, 40
    support from, 41
    training to become, 112
    Instructional SMEs
    description of, 9, 12
    roles and responsibilities of, 62–63
    skills of, 63
Instructional systems development. See ISD
Instructor's guides, 112–113
ISD
    after-work overview of, 121
    background information on, 120
    best practice in, 5
    boot camp to learn about, 106, 120, 131
    definition of, 110, 113
    elements of, 110
    getting started in, 119–121
    information about, 53, 114
    professionalization of, 117

questions commonly asked about,
    110–114
simplifying of, 106–107
SMEs and, 5, 12–13, 117–121
teaching of, 105–108
ISD From the Ground Up, 109
ISD interest group, 121

J

Jargon, 113–114, 131

K

Kickoff meeting, 53–54, 89
Kirkpatrick, Donald, 111

L

Lack of participation, 98
Lateness, 88–89
Leadership
    committee, 40–42
    demanding behavior versus, 87
    importance of, 57
    performance evaluations based on, 84
    roles and responsibilities, 59
    SMEs who must lead, 88
Learner prerequisites, 114
Learning evaluation, 111
Learning management system, 61, 114
Legal credentials, 4
Level 1 evaluation, 114
Level 2 evaluation, 114
Level 3 evaluation, 114
Location of experience, 19–20

M

Managed committee, 36, 38
Matrix committee, 36
Medical credentials, 4
Meetings
    attendance at, 82–83
    kickoff, 53–54, 89

N

9 Events, 113–114
Non–English-speaking SMEs, 22

O

Objectives, 110–111
Organizational chart, 52
Organizational standing, 26
Original equipment manufacturers, 103
Outside interference or interests, 102–103
Outside SMEs, 49
Oversight group, 64
Overtime, 100

P

Participation
    equalizing of, 128
    lack of, 98
    opportunities for, 128
    outside direction for, 102
Patronizing, 87
PDF files, 72
Performance evaluation criteria
    attitude, 85
    charting of, 80, 83, 91–92
    communication, 82
    content knowledge, 78–80
    cooperation, 84–85
    deadlines, 82
    deliverables, 81–82
    demanding behavior, 87
    example of, 80, 83
    focus, 85
    intangibles, 83–86
    lateness, 88–89
    leadership, 84, 88
    meeting attendance, 82–83
    negative qualities, 86–91
    patronizing attitude, 87
    preparedness, 80–83
    read-and-review process, 81
    rudeness, 88
    supportive attitude, 85
    team player, 84

tech-bound, 89–90
    volunteering, 85
Performance-based objectives, 107
Personality conflicts, 101–102
Pilot testing, 41–42
Preparedness evaluations, 80–83
Prerequisites, 114
Problems/problem solving
    access, 96–97
    availability, 98
    deadlocked committees, 100–101
    file sharing, 99–100
    lack of participation, 98
    outside interference or interests,
        102–103
    personality conflicts, 101–102
    scheduling conflicts, 97–98
    technological inequities, 99–100
Process-related deliverables, 72–73
Process-related SMEs, 6
Project
    details of, 52–53
    planning of, 13
    scale of, 34, 61
    timeline for, 13
Project management plan, 52
Project start, formula for success in
    background materials, 53
    contact and communication
        information, 51
    first outreach, 50–51
    kickoff meeting, 53–54, 89
    overview of, 49–50
    project details, 52–53
    roles and responsibilities, 51–52

Q

Qualifications
    description of, 3
    scoring system for, 20–21

R

Range-of-experience committee, 37–38
Reaction evaluation, 111

Read and review criterion, for performance evaluation, 81
Reimbursements, 100
Relevance of content knowledge, 78
Relevance of experience, 17
Reputation, 3
Responsiveness, 126–127
Return-on-investment evaluation, 111–112
Review and revision process, 127
ROI. *See* Return-on-investment evaluation
Roles and responsibilities
    assumptions regarding, 58
    clarifying of, 51
    clarity of, 67
    defining of, 59, 67
    description of, 6
    expectations, 58, 61, 67
    first type of, 119
    functional SMEs, 63–64
    hybrid SMEs, 8–9, 60–61
    identification of, 60
    inflation of, 66
    instructional SMEs, 62–63
    issues related to, 65–67
    list of, 67
    overview of, 57–58
    scope creep, 65–66
    sentinel SMEs, 10–12, 64–65
    technical SMEs, 8, 59–60
Rudeness, 88

S

Safety valve, 54
Scale of project, 34, 61
Schedules
    conflicts with, 97–98
    flexibility in, 127
    meeting of, 134
Scope creep, 65–66
Selection criteria
    communication ability, 21–22
    content-based, 18–20
    depth of experience, 18
    general skills, 21–23
    location of experience, 19–20
    nonmeasurable types of, 25–26

    organizational standing, 26
    relevance of experience, 17
    scoring of, 21, 23–25
    sociability, 23
    summary of, 28–29
    timeliness of experience, 18–19
    training/teaching experience, 20
    writing ability, 22
Seminars, 120
Sentinel SMEs
    characteristics of, 64
    as content knowledge experts, 65
    decision making by, 64
    ISD elements and, 12–13
    roles and responsibilities of, 10–12, 57, 64–65
    skills of, 65
    TSMEs and, 11, 58
SMEs
    benefits of categorizing, 12
    content decisions made by, 132–133
    defining of, 3–4, 6, 113
    in design team, 129–130
    dos and don'ts in working with, 123–134
    getting to know, 125–126
    historical background of, 2
    ignoring of, 130
    in-house, 48, 96
    ISD and, 5, 12–13, 117–121
    performance evaluation criteria for. *See* Performance evaluation criteria
    selection criteria for. *See* Selection criteria
    taking for granted, 130
    transitional resistance, 120–121
    types of, 7–12, 58. *See also specific type*
Sociability, 23
Social media, 89
Software, 100
Supplemental materials, content-related, 22
Synchronous, 114

T

Tangible deliverables, 72–73
Task lists, 74–75

Teaching experience, 20
Team player, 84
Technical SMEs
    characteristics of, 8
    committee structures. *See* Committee(s)
    criteria for becoming, 4
    definition of, 3
    experience of, 3–4
    hybrid SMEs versus, 61
    as instructional SMEs, 62
    ISD elements and, 12
    qualifications of, 3–4
    roles and responsibilities, 8, 59–60
    selection criteria for. *See* Selection
        criteria
    sentinel SME and, 11, 58
    skills of, 60
    Technology
    inequities in, 99–100
    reimbursement for purchase of, 100
    SME use of, performance evaluation
        affected by, 89–90
Terminology, 113–114
Time availability, 27–28
Time commitment, 27–28
Timeliness of content knowledge, 79–80
Timeliness of experience, 18–19
To-do lists, 74–75
Training
    academic model of, 118
    in-house SMEs involved in, 48
    SMEs in, 7–12, 117–121
Training environments, 61
Training experience, 20
Training occupations, 5–6

V

Version control
    definition of, 70
    importance of, 71
    numbering systems for, 71–72
    options for, 71–72
    person responsible for, 71
Volunteering, 85

W

Web-based conferencing, 99
Webinars, 120
Workday, 28
Writing ability, 22

HOW TO PURCHASE ASTD PRESS PRODUCTS

All ASTD Press titles may be purchased through ASTD's online store at **www.store.astd.org**.

ASTD Press products are available worldwide through various outlets and booksellers. In the United States and Canada, individuals may also purchase titles (print or eBook) from:

Amazon– www.amazon.com (USA); www.amazon.com (CA)
Google Play– play.google.com/store
EBSCO– www.ebscohost.com/ebooks/home

Outside the United States, English-language ASTD Press titles may be purchased through distributors (divided geographically).

United Kingdom, Continental Europe, the Middle East, North Africa, Central Asia, and Latin America:
Eurospan Group
Phone: 44.1767.604.972
Fax: 44.1767.601.640
Email: eurospan@turpin-distribution.com
Web: www.eurospanbookstore.com
For a complete list of countries serviced via Eurospan please visit www.store.astd.org or email publications@astd.org.

South Africa:
Knowledge Resources
Phone: +27(11)880-8540
Fax: +27(11)880-8700/9829
Email: mail@knowres.co.za
Web: http://www.kr.co.za
For a complete list of countries serviced via Knowledge Resources please visit www.store.astd.org or email publications@astd.org.

Nigeria:
Paradise Bookshops
Phone: 08033075133
Email: paradisebookshops@gmail.com
Website: www.paradisebookshops.com

Asia:
Cengage Learning Asia Pte. Ltd.
Email: asia.info@cengage.com
Web: www.cengageasia.com
For a complete list of countries serviced via Cengage Learning please visit www.store.astd.org or email publications@astd.org.

India:
Cengage India Pvt. Ltd.
Phone: 011 43644 1111
Fax: 011 4364 1100
Email: asia.infoindia@cengage.com

For all other countries, customers may send their publication orders directly to ASTD. Please visit: **www.store.astd.org**.